IMAGES
of America

Old Sebec Lake

SEBEC LAKE!
Season 1911.

Steamer Waban

CAPT. GEO. P. THOMPSON.

Will make Regular Trips
To the Head of Sebec Lake and Return,

Commencing Saturday, June 24, '11

AS FOLLOWS:

The Steamer leaves Greeley's Landing Daily, (Sundays excepted) at 8 A. M. Returning, leaves Head of Lake at 4 P. M. Sundays, leaves Greeley's Landing at 9 o'clock A. M. and Head of Lake at 4 P. M.

Commencing Saturday, JULY 1,
STEAMER MAKES TWO TRIPS PER DAY,
leaving Greeley's Landing at 8 A. M. and 2 P. M., and the Head of Lake at 9.30 A. M. and 4 P. M.

FARE, Each Way,   25 CENTS.

Special Trips for One or Four Persons, $2.00; all over, 50c each. The Price of STEAMER LINWOOD for Fishing Parties is $5.00 PER DAY.

F. D. Barrows, Printer, Foxcroft.

IMAGES of America
OLD SEBEC LAKE

Dorothy A. Blanchard

ARCADIA

First published 1997
Copyright © Dorothy A. Blanchard, 1997

ISBN 0-7524-0273-0

Published by Arcadia Publishing,
an imprint of the Chalford Publishing Corporation,
One Washington Center, Dover, New Hampshire 03820.
Printed in Great Britain

Library of Congress Cataloging-in-Publication Data applied for

OTHER PUBLICATIONS BY DOROTHY A. BLANCHARD:
"Into the Heart of Maine: A Look at Dexter's Franco-American Community." *Maine Historical Society Quarterly*, Vol. 33, No. 1 (Summer 1993).

Images of America: *Along the Damariscotta*. Arcadia, 1995.

Dedicated to the memory of
Adin A. Green (1908–1996)
Stuart E. Hayes (1922–1996)
Guy Robert "Bob" Weatherbee (1919–1997)

Contents

Introduction		7
Acknowledgments		8
1.	Willimantic	9
2.	Head of the Lake	27
3.	The Big Lake	49
4.	Greeley's Landing	77
5.	Bowerbank and the Lower Lake	95
6.	Sebec Village	111
Bibliography		128

"I love thy shores of forest green,
The birch, the fir, the pine;
Thy shaded groves, I rest serene
As neath them I recline.

Thy cooling wave, and gentle breeze
Are refuge from the heat;
And sunshine days beneath thy trees
Make summer joys complete . . ."

From "Sebec in Summer," a poem written in 1926 by H.F. Huse, a Dover-Foxcroft clergyman. Photograph: Biri Fay.

Introduction

In 1859, when Bryant & Keating's horseboat made its first trip to the head of Sebec Lake, probably no one realized it was the beginning of an era. But as horses gave way to steam and transportation was revolutionized, a fascinating and colorful period of history unfolded along this 12-mile stretch of water. It was an age of steamboats and log haulers, spool mills and sporting camps, band concerts and buckboard rides. It was a time when men hunted caribou for the Boston market and strapped on snowshoes to tend 30-mile traplines. There were new ventures and old-fashioned philosophies, hard work and simple pleasures, and as always, good times and hard times.

Of course, human activity around the lake began much earlier. For generations, various Wabanaki tribes had used the lake as part of an inland water route to the north. When the first settlers moved in during the early part of the nineteenth century, they established mills at the outlet of the lake and at Wilson Stream, Bog Brook, and Mill Brook. The small villages that grew up around the mills prospered for awhile, but with economies heavily dependent on natural resources, they were vulnerable to the uncertainties of weather, markets, and transportation. Severe cycles of prosperity and economic depression were felt by the lake towns, whose fortunes were tied to timber, farm crops, granite, and slate.

The years 1860–1950 brought many changes to Willimantic, Bowerbank, and Sebec, and even to the lake itself, as it made the transition from a working lake to one focused on recreation. It is fortunate that the art of photography developed during this period, and that so much of the era has been captured on film. These old photographs not only document the period's changes, they also bring to life some of the people and events associated with them, and they serve to remind us of the rich heritage that is part of Sebec Lake. It is quite a legacy.

Dorothy A. Blanchard,
February 1997

Acknowledgments

The research for this book was accomplished with the cooperation and genuine helpfulness of a great number of people. A long list of credits goes out to local residents, summer residents, and historians who have loaned photographs, shared information, and told stories to help with its publication. I was overwhelmed, not only by the amount of material available, but by the number of people willing—even eager—to make a contribution. This project confirmed what I already knew, that Sebec Lake is very dear to the hearts of those who spend time there. And the care with which so many people have preserved its past is extraordinary. Sebec Lake is a special place. I hope I have helped to convey a sense of its history.

Over 500 photographs—some from historical archives, many others from private collections and family albums—were examined for the book. Each one represents a small portion of history treasured by its owner. My sincere thanks to the following people who contributed photographs: Biri Fay, John Parsons, Stuart Hayes, Jerry & Amanda Packard, Gordon James, Adin & Kathryn Green, Cali Turner, John Arnold, Carolyn Stecher, Binnie & George Chase, Mary Stuart, Sydney Pratt, Eloise Stevens, Borestone Mountain Sanctuary, Dick Jordan, Elizabeth Brown, John Redman, Gini Redman, Georganne Dow, Dr. Ed Wyman Jr., Sam Lamb Jr., John Lamb, Peg Padgett, Elaine Balsley, Clair Hall, Dave Raymond, Madelyn Betts, Tim Merrill, Francis & Marion Smith, Ellen Keenan, Eva Mountain, Bob & Ruth Weatherbee, Margaret Goulette, Dot Warren, Priscilla White, Des Coy, Frank & Virgie Allen, George Levensalor, Neil Soule, Dave Smith, Lois Reynolds, Frances Tucker, Rodney & Eunice Preble, Heather Crozier, Arlene Weymouth, Susan Small, Marion Doore, Madeline Acker, Elsie Watters, Roscoe Lamson, Dave Mallett, Mac Blanchard, Betty Ellis, and the Sebec Historical Society.

A very special thanks is extended to Beth Cawley and Steve Rainsford, who spent the better part of two summers keeping me supplied with an enormous amount of material—and still kept coming up with more! And to Russell Carey who allowed me to use material from his unpublished master's thesis *3,750,000,000 Perfect Wooden Spools*.

Thanks also to Sam Shepherd Jr., Mildred Levensalor, Jean Rich, Ruth Dauphinee, Ann Jackson, Kay Gourley, John & Barbara Glover, Beth Snyder, Jan Waterman, Emily Thornton, Martha Rollins, Bruce Gerard, Chris Balsley, Barbara Howard, Carlson Williams, Nathan & Elaine Hall, Earl Brawn, John Wiles, Neil & Patsy Mallett, and Nils Peterson who provided information, leads, advice, and know-how.

Much of the text on the following pages is oral history. Several interviews were completed with people who grew up, worked, or vacationed around Sebec Lake many years ago. Their stories add another dimension to the photographs as they illuminate everyday life in a way no other source can. There are wonderful storytellers around Sebec Lake. I was fortunate enough to spend several enjoyable hours with Christine Packard, Adin Green, George Moore, Jean Fay, Francis Smith, Mary Stuart, Eloise Stevens, Roscoe Lamson, Marion Doore, and Albert Preble. It was an enriching experience. Thank you all for sharing your memories and for contributing so much to this book. Storytelling is alive and well at Sebec Lake. May it always be so.

One
Willimantic

Looking north from Packard's Camps, one can easily understand why natural resources have come to play such an important role in Willimantic's development and economy. Not only do forests blanket the entire region, but low-lying mountains, many ponds and brooks, the Big Wilson and Ship Pond Streams, and several miles of shoreline around Sebec Lake also fall within the town's boundaries. Timber and forest products, fish and game—including the sporting camps and tourist trade that grew up around those resources—and the nineteenth-century discoveries of granite and slate have all contributed to boom-and-bust periods in Willimantic's history. Just north of the town line, the familiar shape of Borestone rises as a prominent feature of the landscape. The mountain, although it is located some distance from the lake, has stood silently on the horizon and has provided a fitting backdrop for the thousands of photographs that have been taken of Sebec Lake over the years. Climbed by countless residents and tourists, and photographed from every angle, Borestone, with its own unique story, deserves to be included as part of the lake's history. (Biri Fay.)

T8 R8 (first called Howard, then Willimantic) was originally part of the "wildlands" in the district of Maine which were offered for sale by the Commonwealth of Massachusetts to help defray its Revolutionary War debt. During the first half of the nineteenth century, much land speculation occurred in the township as large tracts were bought and sold for timber stumpage. John Greeley, Peter Brawn, and a few other settlers arrived during that time, but the sale of homesteading lots was not promoted until the 1850s, when Abijah Howard and others acquired title to most of the land. The few families who carved out homes in the wilderness west of Sebec Lake found plenty of timber and fertile land along the streams, and over the next twenty years the population gradually increased, so that by 1870, when the first U.S. Census was taken, 173 people lived in the township. The view in the photograph above is from Monson Hill, looking toward the lake. The amount of cleared land reveals how successful the early settlers were in cutting back the forest for their farms and fields. Although the photograph is not dated, it is obvious that these views existed many years ago. The panorama is obscured today by the forest which has already reclaimed some of the pastures and tilled fields of Willimantic's pioneers. The small white building in the center of the photograph is the school, which is still standing across from the cemetery at Hart's Corner. (Cali Turner.)

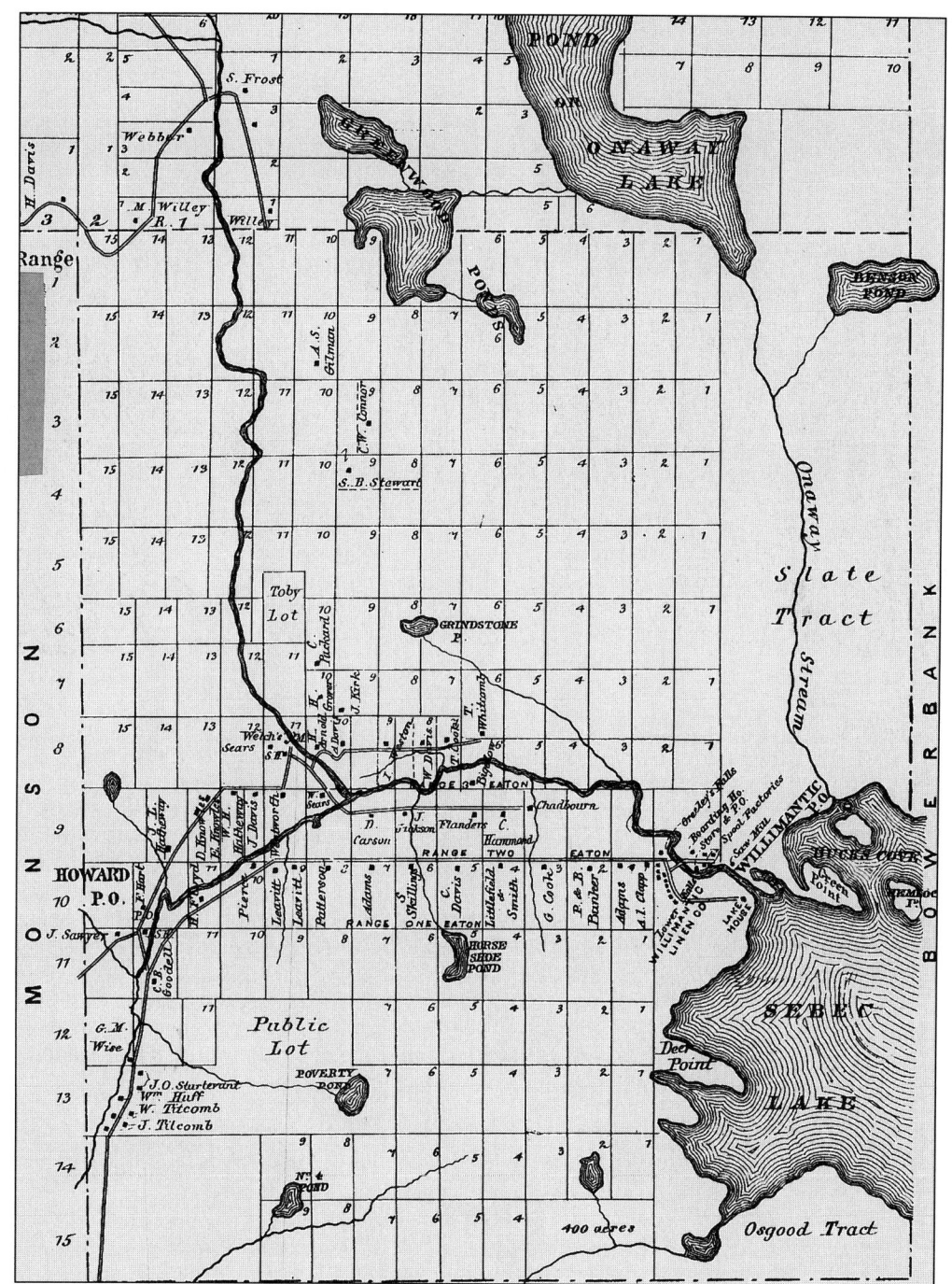

This map of Howard is from Colby's *Atlas of Piscataquis County* (1882). It traces the course of Wilson Stream flowing down from the north, and clearly shows the influence of that body of water on the industry and settlement of the area that was to become Willimantic. Sawmills established at Greenwood (later Tobey) Falls and at Greeley's Falls near the mouth of the stream encouraged people to settle, but not until the spool mill arrived did the town's population increase dramatically.

11

In 1879 James and Sprague Adams, owners of large tracts of land in the township, sold 173 acres at Greeley's Falls to the Willimantic Linen Company of Willimantic, Connecticut, "plus all the white birch standing on the proprietor's land in the township," according to Loring's *History of Piscataquis County*. The company immediately set to work building a mill for splitting out spool timber, as well as drying sheds, shops, and a boarding house (center) on the north bank of Wilson Stream. (Steve Rainsford.)

At first only rough blocks were produced, but in 1886 a spool mill was added. The finished product was transported by horse-drawn wagons 14 miles to Howard Siding in Abbot for rail shipment to the thread factory in Connecticut. The wagon route wound through the stark landscape of the red-painted company houses on the south bank of the stream, and past the small white homes of other villagers (center background) on the main road. (Cali Turner.)

The Salmon Pool, Willimantic, Me.

Another view of the company houses, taken from the lower falls, includes the white building which served as a combination store/post office/dance hall, and was the focal point of activity for the busy little town. In her book, *Birch Stream and Other Poems*, Dover poet Anna Boynton Averill comments on the changes that took place at the falls in Willimantic:

> It was here when the lonely hills were still,
> Before they built the busy mill,
> That we came in the autumn bright and chill
> And climbed these rocks at our own sweet will.
>
> But now roofs nestle among the trees,
> The smoke of traffic is in the breeze;
> The whistle screams, and electric lights
> Flash fron the darkness of winter nights . . .
>
> Did the little red hamlet grow in a dream
> Among the mountains, beside the stream?
> Behold how they shelter it, close and near,
> As if they still loved it and held it dear:
> —Shall we sorrow then if the mountain glen
> Holds in its warm heart homes for men?

13

The mill, which began operating in January 1880, was very modern, and included both a sprinkler system and the first electric lights in the county. After the addition of the spool mill, about fifty men were employed at the plant itself, with another seventy-five engaged during the winter, cutting and hauling timber to the factory. Thousands of cords of white birch were cut each year in the area between Sebec Lake and Lake Onawa to supply the saws at the mill on Wilson Stream. The wooden spools manufactured had to be constructed to exact specifications for the thread company, depending upon the type of material to be wound on them. This required both sophisticated machinery and skilled employees. The company was proud of its modern plant (one slate-roofed building is still standing) and good community relations ensured a steady work force. With the arrival of the Willimantic Linen Company, the population of the township more than doubled, and the period between 1880 and 1903 was the most active in the town's history. In 1881 T8 R8 was incorporated as the town of Howard, named after Abijah Howard, the former land owner. But just two years later its name was changed to Willimantic, for the company that had transformed the small settlement into a bustling community. (Cali Turner.)

The boom was short-lived, however, for in 1898 the company merged with twelve other thread companies to become the American Thread Company. In 1902, after building a large spool mill in Milo which had closer access to rail transportation, American Thread closed its Willimantic plant and moved forty employees and their families to the new site. By 1910, Willimantic's population had declined to 271. After the mill closed, the town's economy relied mostly on farming and lumbering, and the area at the Falls once again became a pleasant spot for fishing and picnicking. (Beth Cawley.)

In 1903 Bill Earley purchased the mill boarding house. He ran it as a hotel for a number of years, while also continuing to operate the store and dance hall. He eventually bought the remaining land and buildings vacated by the American Thread Company, and gradually added housekeeping cabins to accommodate more guests. Earley's Camps were a popular destination for sportsmen for over fifty years. (Beth Cawley.)

There were hard times in Willimantic after the spool mill closed, and several people sought employment outside the area. Ervin Green (left) moved his family to California for three years in the 1920s to work clearing land for a reservoir outside San Francisco. His son Adin (right), who was fourteen at the time, earned 45¢ an hour for leading a ten-horse pack train. It was a responsible job and "good money in those days." The photos they sent back home seem to prove the men were also adept at providing the family with fresh fish. (Cali Turner.)

The Canadian Pacific Railway slices through the northern Willimantic wilderness and crosses Ship Pond Stream near the outlet of Lake Onawa. The wooden bridge, built in 1887, was the longest and highest structure of its kind on the CPR line which cut across Maine, linking the Maritime Provinces with the rest of Canada. The steel trestle shown here replaced the original in 1896. Looming in the distance, Borestone Mountain rises abruptly from Lake Onawa, its unique shape a familiar sight to travelers in this part of Maine. (Gordon James.)

These girls from Camp Wichitee on Sebec Lake scramble over the ledges near the top of Borestone, c. 1925, in what was an annual event for the campers. The mountain is small (1947 feet high) but it is rugged enough to please hikers of all ages. It's interesting geological features were the subject of a doctoral study done by Dr. Shailer S. Philbrick in the 1930s. His detailed explanation of how the mountain was formed is displayed in a library named for him at the main lodge on Borestone. (Stuart Hayes.)

Borestone's bald peaks can be seen for miles around, and have appeared on maps since Joseph Chadwick first sketched them while surveying a route to Quebec in 1764. The view from the summit includes a heavily forested area of southern Piscataquis County, and was used as a fire lookout for many years. The lookout cabin was manned by Tom Katon, who lived in a camp high up on the mountain overlooking Greenwood Pond, and who climbed to the summit (on crutches!) to perform his duties as fire warden. These young hikers from Sebec Lake's south shore are photographed at the lookout in the 1920s. From left to right are Elizabeth "Bill" Redman (Brown), John Redman, and Arnold Norcross. (Gini Redman.)

Posing for a photograph in 1917 are Henry D. Moore, his wife, Mary, and their grandchildren, Karlene and Terris. The Moore family was part of a fascinating chapter of Borestone Mountain's history involving the fox ranch and fish hatchery that operated there from 1916 to 1930. The Moores began coming to their cabin on Benson Pond before 1900, soon after the Canadian Pacific Railway made the northern wilderness more accessible. Their youngest son, Robert T., loved the area, and in 1908 started buying parcels of cut-over woodland high on Borestone Mountain. Henry D. cautioned his son about investing in such wasteland, but Robert dreamed of starting a fox ranch at his mountain retreat. By 1917, Robert T. Moore had built a log cabin, a new 1 1/4-mile access road to the ponds, and began to construct buildings and pens for up to two hundred foxes. (Borestone Mountain Sanctuary.)

An alpine environment was thought to produce superior furs, and the location of the ranch at Sunrise, Midday, and Sunset Ponds was ideal. The main lodge occupied by the Moore family was situated near the outlet of the upper pond, while the fox ranch and fish hatchery were near Sunrise Pond. Part of the ranch can be seen in the photograph above. The animals' behavior was monitored in manned observation towers (the white buildings, in the upper left.) (Dave Raymond.)

Fox farms were common in the 1920s, due to the popularity of black furs in women's fashions, and the industry flourished in Maine and eastern Canada. The first breeding stock of silver-black foxes came from Prince Edward Island, and Robert T. Moore spent four years building up his stock to fifty breeding pairs, so that there would be an annual output of one hundred pelts for the New York fur market. Mr. Moore hired George Falconer, a Prince Edward Islander with ranching experience, as superintendent. Mr. Falconer lived on the mountain year-round with his family, and provided the expert care needed for the production of quality pelts and championship breeding stock. The pelts of prize-winning silver-blacks could bring several hundred dollars apiece, and the winners of champion live fox shows received thousands. Careful attention to genetics and mating details at the Borestone ranch produced more than half the Grand Show Champion foxes in the country during the decade of the 1920s. In the above photograph, Mr. Moore holds "Borestone Reid," the grand champion of the Montreal and Boston Live Fox Shows in 1920. By 1930, over-production of black foxes, change in women's fashions, and the Depression all led to a decline in fox farming. Robert T. Moore eventually leased the property to Thompson L. Guernsey, of Dover-Foxcroft, who used it to entertain business guests in conjunction with his lodge on Sebec Lake. Although R.T. Moore willed the property to the National Audubon Society upon his death in 1958, his son Terris had life-tenancy, and was often seen flying his float plane in and out of Midday Pond. (Eloise Stevens.)

This lumber camp near Greenwood Pond is typical of those scattered throughout the Maine woods in the early twentieth century. Willimantic's forests, both hardwood and softwood, have been extensively harvested over the years. Before the turn of the century the town's timber industry was its chief economic asset. According to the 1891 State Assessor's Report, Willimantic had the highest valuation of logs and lumber of any town in Piscataquis County. (Gordon James.)

Bert Knowles cut off the pine grove on his land in the early 1920s and yarded the logs to the edge of Wilson Stream below Tobey Falls. This became the last log drive on Wilson Stream. Twenty years later Adin Green, Rex Turner, George Young, and Max Shaw sent 350 cords of pulp down the stream, the last drive of its kind, and the final chapter in the long history of driving timber at the head of the lake. (Gordon James.)

Combining steam power, horsepower, and manpower, George Titcomb and his son Ivory manufacture clapboards at their farm soon after the turn of the century. The circular clapboard saw was invented by two Brunswick men, and it soon became a welcome addition to small woodworking operations throughout the state, although it probably required Ivory's mechanical abilities to keep it running smoothly. (Gordon James.)

Ivory Titcomb was born in 1876, when Willimantic was still an unorganized township. He was a well-known hunter, who claimed to have shot the last caribou in this section of Maine when he was twelve years old. Caribou, once plentiful in the area, suddenly disappeared before the turn of the century, apparent victims of human encroachment on their habitat. In this photograph Ivory Titcomb poses with an 8-point buck. (Gordon James.)

The rural nature of the town made the Willimantic Grange, No. 415, one of the most active organizations in the community. Grange meetings and social gatherings, such as the one pictured above, were held at the Town Hall and usually drew a large crowd. This photograph appears to have been taken in the early 1900s, well before the time when farming ceased to be an important occupation in Willimantic. The Grange became inactive about 1950. (Gordon James.)

Willimantic's schoolhouse #3, on the road to Sebec Lake, was built c. 1890, when the spool mill was booming and the town's population had reached its peak of 446. By holding entertainments and sales, the children and their teacher soon raised enough money to purchase a bell. But before a belfry could be built, the mill closed, families moved away, and the town began to die. The schoolhouse survived, but without its belfry. In 1919 Miss Harriet Crockett, who had helped earn money for the bell as a child, returned to Willimantic to teach, and rallied the community for funds to build the belfry. When the belfry was finally constructed, Scott Cook, the well-known Packard's guide, bronzed and polished the bell and it was finally installed, rescued from the pile of shavings in the Crockett barn where it had been stored for nearly thirty years. (Beth Cawley.)

Not far from the schoolhouse, one of Maine's most famous sculptors maintained a summer home. Charles Eugene Tefft, a native of Brewer, displayed an extraordinary talent at an early age, and during his lifetime created memorable works of art that have become prominent features of many American cities. Busts of Civil War generals Chamberlain, McClellan, and Sheridan, statues of Hannibal Hamlin, Abraham Lincoln, and William McKinley, as well as several war memorials and equestrian statues, adorn public buildings and parks throughout the country. Although his work took him far from his native state, C.E. Tefft loved hunting, fishing and relaxing in Maine, especially in the quiet woods around Willimantic. He is shown here at the Carver cottage on Wilson Stream with the Carvers' daughter, Carolyn. (Carolyn Stecher.)

Among Mr. Tefft's sculptures in the state of Maine is "The Last Drive," a memorial to Luther H. Peirce which stands in a park next to the Bangor Public Library. Commissioned by the Peirce family to create a suitable memorial, Charles Tefft suggested the lumbering theme, since the family was associated with the industry and Bangor was once the lumber capital of the world. The work received high praise for its truthful portrayal of its subject. Mr. Tefft's Willimantic neighbor and assistant sculptor, David Preble, modeled for all three river drivers, as well as for the statue of Hannibal Hamlin, which stands in nearby Norumbega Park. (Carolyn Stecher.)

Lon Arnold was a woodsman, trapper, and one of the last old-time professional market hunters. Born in Monson in 1853, he had the fearless independence of this country's early frontiersmen. He attended school for just six weeks, and said he obtained his education by "listening to others and taking jolts over the thank-you-ma'ams of life." He hunted for a living, providing deer meat for lumber camps and caribou for the Boston market, c. 1870. This was a legitimate occupation in those days which, along with trapping and making maple syrup, earned him a living. His first season he shot twenty-seven caribou and seventeen deer, shipping them to Hyde & Wheeler in Boston for 9 1/2¢ a pound. After market hunting was outlawed (before the turn of the century), Lon Arnold farmed a little, cut birch for American Thread, and continued to trap and guide for Packard's until he was eighty years old. (Carolyn Stecher.)

Lon Arnold's son Walter followed his father into the woods and began to earn a living trapping at an early age. Born and raised in the Willimantic back country, Walter Arnold became one of Maine's most famous trappers and guides. He was the author of several books and manuals on trapping, and was a mail-order dealer in trappers' supplies and scents. A familiar figure at sportsman's shows and trappers' conventions, Walter Arnold became the subject of many articles written about his profession and lifestyle in the Maine woods. (Beth Cawley.)

Later in his life Walter Arnold lived alone at a camp he built on Indian Pond. Walter Arnold's sense of humor and his unique lifestyle generally granted him an audience, and all of his friends especially looked forward to his annual Christmas letter. The following is an excerpt from a letter he wrote soon after he was hospitalized with a blood clot in his leg:

"What am I doing to keep well? Well—after some experience with blood clots and reading about that dreaded Cholesterol and hearing that egg yolks are loaded with the awful stuff I decided a year ago to eat no more yolks, just the whites—will take a chance on them. Now this decision produced problems for me. What the heck to do with the unwanted yolks? I could throw them into the pond and my ever hungry pet suckers would take care of them fast. But those suckers are my friends and clean up every crumb of the table scraps I throw to them—a most convenient and efficient way of disposal. Now of course I would not consider for one moment feeding those good friends anything that was likely to give them hardening of the arteries. I finally decided to burn those death dealers, and since then my stove has been fed a steady diet of egg yolks. However, I have learned that Cholesterol is a wicked, crafty, powerful enemy, not to be made light of. That cussed stuff has been quietly building onto the inside walls of my stovepipe so that now I have only a sluggish draft in my stove and it has become evident that I am now stuck with a chronic case of hardening of the stovepipe." (Author's collection.)

Adin Green (left) and Walter Arnold were guides, trappers, and friends. Each ran a trapline in the heavily wooded area north of Sebec Lake. These Willimantic woodsmen were fond of sharing their knowledge, and entertained generations of Mainers by telling stories and writing articles about their experiences. Adin started trapping in 1926, establishing a 30-mile trapline from Willimantic over the Barren-Chairback Range into the country near Gulf Hagas. Walter's trapline ran south and east of Adin's in the area around Indian Pond. According to Adin, there was an unwritten code about backcountry trapping that said it was "unethical—if not downright unhealthy" to invade another trapper's territory, so the two men rarely met during trapping season, but they kept track of each other nevertheless. Near the spot where the two traplines met grew a large toadstool. Every time the men passed by, they carved their name and the date into it. For two trappers working 30-mile traplines, it was a way to stay in touch. Adin said, "It was our mailbox." (Adin Green.)

Two
Head of the Lake

Several years after Peter Brawn "cleared up an opening" at the mouth of Wilson Stream in 1826, activity at the head of the lake began to increase. The Lake House (now Packard's Camps) attracted loggers, trappers, gum pickers, summer boarders, fishermen, and hunters. Steamboats traveled the channel, and lumbermen drove logs down the stream. In 1900, the area in the photograph above was the site of the first trip by a gasoline-powered motorboat. According to Marlborough Packard, the boat gave "a very discouraging performance." It belonged to Angus and Dave Campbell and ran from Packard's Landing to the mouth of Wilson Stream during its only run. Wet batteries abruptly halted its maiden voyage, and the boat had to be towed back. (John Parsons.)

The value of this photograph lies in its depiction of the horse treadmill, used in this case to thresh grain. The same mechanism was used to power the first commercial boat on Sebec Lake in 1859. G.E.S. Bryant and Thomas Keating equipped an old ferryboat with a horse treadmill connected to paddlewheels. As the horses walked, the boat was propelled—slowly, but if conditions were just right, the boat could navigate the length of the lake in four hours. Bryant & Keating advertised daily trips during July and August for "sporting and blueberrying." For 50¢, passengers could spend a pleasant day at the head of the lake fishing Wilson Stream, blueberrying on Granite Mountain, or, as newspaper ads suggested, just "enjoying Nature spread out in unsurpassed loveliness." Such activities appealed to crowds of local people, and Bryant & Keating's excursions became very popular—so popular, in fact, that two years later Ansel Crockett and Lathrop Jones introduced the *Favorite*, a steam-powered paddle wheeler capable of carrying three hundred passengers. This boat also was successful, and it not only launched the career of Captain Crockett, who went on to play the leading role in steamboating on the lake for the next half-century, but provided the incentive for other entrepreneurs to begin new ventures at Sebec Lake. (Gordon James.)

In 1868, Captain Crockett built the *Rippling Wave*. Made of lumber cut in Bowerbank, she was a 90-foot sidewheeler with spacious cabins, a full hurricane deck, and the capacity to carry five hundred passengers. The *Rippling Wave* was constructed by Major Bigney, who also built the Moosehead Lake steamboats, *Fairy of the Lake* and *Governor Coburn*. Note the large pile of wood on the shore, which was needed to fire the boiler of the *Rippling Wave*. (Beth Cawley.)

In 1866, William Blethen and George Gilman, of Dover, built a large hotel near the mouth of Wilson Stream. A few years later the Lake House was bought by Captain Crockett and his wife, Sarah, who ran it along with his steamboat excursions to the head of the lake. Listed among the attractions at the Lake House during those years was "the bewitching game of croquet." (Beth Cawley.)

When Burton Marlborough Packard bought the Lake House from Captain Crockett in 1894, he inherited what his son Marlborough described as "a sort of hotel in the rough." The exterior walls were single-boarded, exposing the rough framework inside and allowing daylight to show through in several places. Thin partitions separated the bedrooms, the floors were uncarpeted, and there was a dilapidated front porch, but just four years later, the hotel had become the well-kept building in the photograph above. Unscreened windows, kerosene lamps, wood stoves (downstairs only), an outdoor toilet, and water carried from the spring were the amenities in those early years. Gradually, running water and a new kitchen were added, and the hotel began to attract summer boarders, fishermen, river drivers, lumbermen, and blueberry pickers. There were political rallies and field days, Sunday school picnics, and groups of people touring on bicycles. Although some of those groups brought their own lunches and provided little business for the hotel, everyone was welcome, and news of the hospitality at the Lake Hotel spread. The group of people sitting on the porch of the newly renovated hotel are, from left to right, Harvey Hurd, (who was the "hired man"), Mrs Shaffer (a guest), Mrs. Etta Day Packard, Mr. B.M. Packard, and their son Marlborough. The man with the bicycle is Bill Earley, later the proprietor of Earley's Camps. (Beth Cawley.)

The bowling alley with its refreshment counter and cigar case was a popular place among the berry pickers, tenting parties, and men who worked in the spool mill. After the mill closed and most of the local business disappeared, the front part of the building became the store where supplies of all kinds could be purchased. (Beth Cawley.)

Etta and B.M. Packard posed for this photograph with their children: Marlborough (far left), Dorothy (middle left), Mary (center), Royal (center right), and Burton Nessmuc (far right). The children attended Willimantic grade schools, then East Maine Conference Seminary in Bucksport, a school their father attended. Burton joined his father in the business, but all of the Packard children were influenced by their upbringing on Sebec Lake, and all returned to the lake at various times in their lives. (Beth Cawley.)

31

Dorothy Packard loved animals, and as a child, she convinced her father to let her raise twin Holstein-Friesian calves born at the Packard farm. She raised them and trained them to the yoke, so they could haul heavy loads on sleds. Many of the goods used by the hotel arrived by steamboat, and the oxen became useful draft animals, hauling grain and other supplies from the beach to the barn. (Beth Cawley.)

This wagon pulled by "Pat" and "Tig" was used by the guides to transport guests to various fishing sites around the area. It was possible to go by buckboard to Lake Onawa, and to be driven to some of the open fishing stretches above the falls on Wilson Stream. (Beth Cawley.)

After the spool mill closed in Willimantic, B.M. Packard closed the bowling alley and refreshment counter, and concentrated on running his establishment strictly as a sporting camp. Mr. Packard mainly advertised in the Bangor & Aroostook Railroad's annual publication, *In the Maine Woods*. He also represented the railroad at the New York Sportsman's Show at Madison Square Garden from 1908 to 1917. B.M. Packard is second from right. (Beth Cawley.)

Guides were an important part of the early success of Packard's sporting camp. Their good nature, and especially their story-telling, made them camp favorites. Guide Scott Cook looks as if he thoroughly enjoys his work. According to Marlborough Packard, Scott "caught more fish, shot more deer, and worked in more lumber camps than one could imagine,"—all on the front porch. Once, after relating some of his exploits to a stranger, the man introduced himself as the new game warden. Scott, recovering quickly, said, "Shake hands with the biggest liar in the State of Maine." (Beth Cawley.)

33

Sam McKenney, another popular guide, serves up a camp meal to a party of Boy Scouts tenting at the lake. Sam lived with the Packards for a few years and practically became a member of the family. He worked wherever he was needed—in the store, doing the repair work, building cabins, making furniture, and teaching the Packard children games and camping skills. (Beth Cawley.)

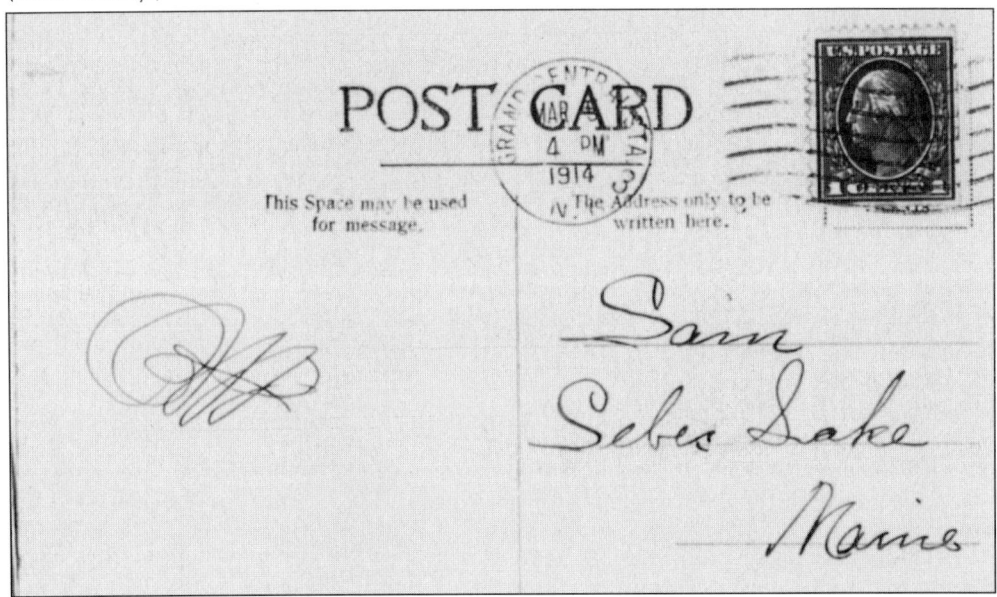

Whenever B.M. Packard went to the Sportsman's Show or to a destination beyond the state of Maine, he always sent Sam McKenney a postcard, signed with his characteristic "BMP," and addressed simply to "Sam, Sebec Lake, Maine." The old guide loved to receive mail—and it always reached him at the correct address. (Beth Cawley.)

34

Dan Neal was famous as an oldtime Maine woodsman. He hunted for the Boston market in the 1870s, guided at Packard's, worked as a blacksmith at the spool mill in Willimantic, and made canoes, snowshoes, and moccasins in his spare time. The son of a circuit-riding preacher, and a staunch Democrat, Dan had strong opinions and a hearty backwoods philosophy. He was convinced that money, laziness, and women contributed to most of society's ills: "The world has become so corroded with hypocrisy and flub-dub that it's going to take a spiritual hurricane to get men and women back to normal." And his favorite theme: "The world will continue to go to the dogs until women get back to the barrel of flour . . ." (Jerry and Amanda Packard.)

Harvey Hurd holds up a nice catch after a spring fishing trip with some guests at the Lake Hotel. Harvey was one of the original hired men and guides to work for B.M. Packard. He did the barn chores, fed the livestock, milked the cows, and was also a good man with an axe. In the first winter of the hotel's operation he single-handedly cut over a large section of woods behind the hotel (what is now field). Harvey was an excellent boatman and had wonderful stories to tell of his younger days working on ocean-going sailing vessels. He was one of the best fishermen and storytellers in camp. Marlborough Packard wrote a caption under this photograph in a Packard family album: "Wooden barrels on the dock were filled with sand to provide some stability when getting out of the canoes. But when the portly gentleman in the bow stepped out, he pulled the barrel over and both went into the water. Although he could not swim, he was so fat, he floated, and as he drifted downstream, he was, with difficulty, caught with a boathook and towed ashore. Harvey, his guide, in describing the incident said, 'If the big lummox hadn't thrashed around so much, I would have jumped aboard him and paddled him ashore!' " (Beth Cawley.)

PACKARD'S CAMPS

SOMETIMES CALLED LAKE HOTEL AND COTTAGES

A Fishing Place for Real Sportsmen

22 Cabins and Cottages. All with Bathrooms. Hot and Cold Spring Water. Central Dining Room. Open Fires.

Salmon Fishing

on Sebec Lake, in May, June and September, is positively good and the Fly Fishing for Black Bass is claimed by many to equal Maine's most famous Bass Lakes. There are a number of nearby Ponds and Streams where the Trout Fishing is always good.

You can live in a cabin and take meals at the house, an ideal place for families to spend the summer. Tennis court for use of guests. Post-office and telephone in the house. Steaks, Chops and Fish broiled over a Charcoal broiler. Booklet and rates on request.

B. M. PACKARD & SON, SEBEC LAKE, MAINE

Telegraph Address: Sebec Lake, Maine.   In Piscataquis County

By the 1920s, Burton N. Packard had joined his father in the day to day operation of the camps, and the business continued expanding. This ad in the 1932 *In the Maine Woods* indicates how much the business had grown. Twenty-two cabins with bathrooms, a tennis court, home-cooked meals, a telephone and post office located in the hotel, and several boats for fishing offered guests plenty to do.

37

Every Fourth of July, beginning in the 1920s, the entire crowd at Packard's Camps (as it was now called) assembled for a day of celebration and fun. During the 1926 celebration, B.M. Packard gave a patriotic address, and there were fireworks, games, contests, and the "Horribles Parade"—a contest in which all of the employees paraded around the yard dressed in horrible costumes (above) while the guests provided the prizes. (Beth Cawley.)

Pictured at Packard's in 1936 are, from left to right, guides Bill Gourley, Duane Whitten, and Coney Packard, longtime guest Charlie Miller, and guides Burton N. Packard and Henry Foster. In one of many courtships begun at Packard's, Bill Gourley met his future wife, Katherine, who also worked at the camps in the 1930s. They married, and later purchased Schoodic Lake Camps, which they ran from 1940 to 1971. (Beth Cawley.)

Christine Packard makes lists for supplies while supervising the dining room, kitchen, and housekeeping crews. She first came to work as a waitress at Packard's in 1921. She traveled all day by train from the coast, then nursed a sick horse on the ride through the woods to Sebec Lake, finally arriving at camp after dark. Such a beginning proved to be a good omen, for Christine later married Burton N. Packard, and with her husband managed Packard's Camps for thirty-two years. (Beth Cawley.)

These waitresses enjoy a few minutes on the porch before going to work in the dining room. From left to right are Pearl Sargent, Ada Young, Lola Merrill, unidentified, and Anna Edgecomb. Many young women from Willimantic and the neighboring towns earned their first money waiting on tables or cleaning cabins, and many a romance blossomed between them and the young men who were working or vacationing at the lake. (Sydney Pratt.)

The wharf at Packard's was always busy, as several steamers made it their destination at the head of the lake. The dark-hulled *Linwood*, owned for a few years around the turn of the century by George Thompson, lies at the dock along with the *Helen A*. This smaller boat was originally christened the *Vivian* by her previous owners, the Crocketts. Her new captain, Willie Clarke, renamed the boat. (Biri Fay.)

STEAMER LEOLA,

For Pleasure and Fishing Parties. Telephone 1914-11

Special Trips to Any Part of the Lake. Leave Orders with B.M. Packard

CHAS. H. COY,
Address, Lake Hotel, Sebec Lake, Me.   CAPTAIN and OWNER.

Early in the century a young man named Harry Coy, discouraged from a failed business venture, (he invested in a California racehorse,) began working in the woods around Sebec Lake until he had enough money to buy his first boat. The 35 foot *Leola*, a little steamer he bought from future rival Willie Clarke, began a career that would make his name synonymous with transportation on Sebec Lake. (George Levensalor.)

The *Favorite*, the second steamer on the lake to be so named, was put in service around 1900. Sharpie-built, with a flat bottom and nearly vertical sides, she had a fantail stern and was 33 feet long. The *Favorite* operated only a few years, however, as a spark from the smokestack ignited a fire which burned her at the wharf in Willimantic in 1912. (Beth Cawley.)

Charles Crockett, a son of Captain Ansel Crockett of Sebec, waits for passengers to board the *Favorite* at Packard's Landing. Captain Charles, like his father and brother, Fred, operated steamboats on the lake for several years. In the early 1900s, Charles provided a charter service for guests at Packard's who wished to go on excursions or private fishing trips. (Beth Cawley.)

In 1904, Ira Doore, an East Dover farmer, bought a cottage on the bank of Wilson Stream. His family loved the camp, but getting there involved a 25-mile journey by road. After finishing the evening farm chores and packing into their wagon all the food, clothing, and supplies necessary (including kerosene for the lamps), the Doores would leave for the camp, sometimes arriving at the lake just as dawn was breaking. (Marion Doore.)

Ira and Harriet Doore take daughters Marion, Marjorie, and Verlie for a boat ride near their camp. Mr. Doore bought the rowboat in 1908 from B.M. Packard for $15. It was typical of small boats used on the lake before the advent of outboard motors. To make her daughters more comfortable, Mrs. Doore sewed pillows so the little girls could nap. (Marion Doore.)

For several years the Doore family made the overland journey to "Mountain Home," their cottage nestled into the side of Granite Mountain. Eventually they bought property closer to their farm at Parsons' Landing, selling their camp in 1916. The new owners were two young ladies just graduated from nursing school: Henrietta Carver (a niece of B.M. Packard's) and her friend, Harriett Balcom. Their joint ownership lasted just a short time, however, for Miss Balcom soon bought the Colonel Mayo cottage with plans to start a girls' camp. Mrs. Carver, whose husband, William (Josh) Carver, was a young naval officer serving in the Far East, renamed the camp "Lotus Lodge." It is known as the Breen cottage today. (Marion Doore.)

Highland Cottage also sat on the side of Granite Mountain not far from the Carver cottage. It burned in October 1947 as flames raced through the woods during one of Maine's driest seasons on record. The fire apparently started on the power line, and was spotted at night by Christine Packard, who alerted Willimantic firemen. The entire town turned out to fight the blaze, which at one point looked as if it would claim everything from Packard's to the Castle. Firetrucks were driven onto the sandbar, and by starting backfires, the men were able to eventually control the flames. Highland Cottage, owned by the Packard family, as well as an outbuilding to the Carver cottage next door, were the only casualties. (Beth Cawley.)

John F. Webber was a Broadway actor who enjoyed hunting and fishing at Sebec Lake. A friendly man, he was popular among cottage owners and guests at Packard's. Known especially for his role as Father Whalen in *Abie's Irish Rose*, John Webber played over 1,000 consecutive performances of that production in the early 1920s (an American record at the time). (Carolyn Stecher.)

Walter Greene owned two camps on Wilson Stream between Packard's and the Castle. A Broadway actor and Maine guide, Mr. Greene became one of the pioneers of the Appalachian Trail in Maine. Greene planned the route from the Gulf Hagas area to Blanchard, offering hikers a footpath through an open, mature forest, panoramic views from the Barren-Chairback Range, and interesting geological features such as Slugundy Falls and Little Wilson Gorge. His pioneering efforts and dedication to the Maine section of the 2,000-mile footpath led him to become the first president of the newly formed Maine Appalachian Trail Club in 1935. (Beth Cawley.)

Walter Greene and Johnny Webber provide some entertainment with the seat of a two-holer they found in the woods. Stories still circulate today about moonshine being distilled on the mountain behind the camps, and of the rollicking good times that took place along Wilson Stream during Prohibition. Apparently not everyone was delighted with the home-brew, however, as some guests were seen emptying their glasses over the porch rail when their host disappeared into the kitchen! (Beth Cawley.)

Margaret Arnold and her two sons, Malcolm (left) and Gilman, spend some time at the Arnold camp in the mid-1920s. The camp, still in the Arnold family, was built before the turn of the century by the boys' grandfather, John F. Arnold, who brought the building materials by buckboard from his home in Foxcroft. (John Arnold.)

A trek to their camp on Buttermilk Pond in the winter was an annual excursion for Burton and Christine Packard. In 1940 the Chase family, owners of Sebecco Lodge, at the mouth of Wilson Stream, accompanied the Packards on their favorite winter hike. From left to right are Christine Packard, Barbara Chase, George Chase III, Jack Dinsmore, B.N. Packard, Charlotte Chase, and George (Thorndike) Chase Jr. (George and Binnie Chase.)

The large camp known as Sebecco Lodge was built by Foxcroft piano manufacturer John F. Hughes, c. 1902, and was frequently used to entertain family and friends. The camp guest book retained by Mr. Hughes' granddaughter, Mary Stuart, records the names of the Arnolds, the Mayos, the Gilmans, Hanna Lane Gray, and Anna Shaw Buck among other prominent local families who called during the camp's first season. Note that the original pier was made of granite blocks, perhaps quarried at the nearby Merrill quarry on Davis Mountain. The ice destroyed the pier soon after it was built. (Mary Stuart.)

The spacious interior of Sebecco Lodge included, of course, a piano manufactured by Hughes & Son. The installation of such a large, heavy object must have required considerable effort, as the camp is not accessible by road and it sits several feet above the level of the lake. The Hughes family sold the camp in 1919 to a Mr. Locke, who accidentally fell off the porch one summer, injuring himself so badly that he eventually lost all interest in the place and sold it to George (Thorndike) Chase Jr. in 1932. (George and Binnie Chase.)

Early spring brought logs tumbling down Wilson Stream, where they were boomed up to wait for steamboats to tow them down the lake. The stream from the Falls to the Castle was often filled with so many logs no boat could pass. Eventually a channel was cut through Glover's Gut to divert the timber away from the main channel. Pictured is Duke Wolf, a young man who lived with the Packard family prior to World War I. (Beth Cawley.)

In this photograph the *Ivy F* draws the attention of a few onshore spectators, c. 1903. The boat was built by Silas D. Leach for Marion Atkins at Greeley's Landing and was 65 feet long, making it the second longest steamer on Sebec Lake (only the original *Rippling Wave* was larger). The boat was later purchased by Colonel Edward J. Mayo and renamed *Waban*. (Dave Raymond.)

Three
The Big Lake

The steamer *Morning Glory* sits at the dock in front of the Grand View Hotel, just above the Narrows, with the Big Lake spread out behind it. From the early days of steamboating, when crowds of people came to pick blueberries on Granite Mountain and tenting parties camped on Jordan Island, this part of the lake has drawn vacationers. Each summer during the last years of the nineteenth century the *Piscataquis Observer* commented on the activity in the Big Lake and assured its readers that the current season was even better than the last: "More people are now enjoying rest and recreation at this resort than for any season. From the Narrows all around the upper lake, white tents dot the shores, peeping out from the forest . . ." Later, fishing trips, picnics on Canoodlin and Gibraltar, hikes to the Ice Caves, and swimming at South Cove beaches provided outdoor entertainment for generations of Sebec Lakers spending time at the family camp. (Beth Cawley.)

The calm waters of Buck's Cove belie the amount of activity that took place here before the turn of the century. A slate quarry and fish hatchery operated at the mouth of Ship Pond Stream in the 1870s, and each spring, timber driven down from Lake Onawa piled up in the cove, waiting for steamboats to begin towing the huge booms down the lake. Buck's Cove, named for Benjamin T. Buck, an early Foxcroft settler, is also the watery grave of the steamboat *Marion*, deliberately sunk by her owner, Harry Coy, in 1932. (Biri Fay.)

The Sebec Landlocked Salmon Breeding Works operated at the mouth of Ship Pond Stream from 1873 to 1876. Established by the U.S. Fishery Commission, it was a cooperative effort between that organization and the states of Maine, Massachusetts, and Connecticut, and was "a landlocked salmon egg-taking operation." Its existence was brief, and hatchery records do not indicate why the venture was discontinued. (Beth Cawley.)

The *Rippling Wave* takes on a load of wood at the Howard Slate Company's wharf at the mouth of Ship Pond Stream. In 1870 a group of Bangor men purchased 4,000 acres of land in the northeast corner of T8 R8 (see map on p. 11) hoping to extract a vein of slate discovered there. Doing business as the Howard Slate Company, they constructed buildings for manufacturing slate shingles and built a tramway that extended 1.5 miles to a steamboat landing in Buck's Cove. For a few years in the 1870s, the company shipped slate down the lake to Blethen's (later Greeley's) Landing, where it was loaded onto oxcarts for the trip to Dover. But the slate could not be worked profitably, and sometime before 1880 the company abandoned the business. The same year the Howard Slate Co. began operating, two bills passed the Maine Legislature incorporating the Ship Pond Stream Navigation Company and the Ship Pond Valley Railroad Company. Backed by the same group of men, the navigation company was permitted to construct dams and locks on the stream, and the railroad company was to build a rail line from Sebec Lake to Elliotsville along the valley. No evidence exists that any of these facilities were constructed. Willimantic's other slate quarry near Norton's Corner was run in the early part of this century by the Leighton brothers. Slabs of slate are still visible in the woods at both sites. (Beth Cawley.)

Colonel Harold G. "Pete" Storke and his wife, Edith, bought an old cabin on a small island in the westerly channel to Buck's Cove. They gradually added a boathouse, several other outbuildings, and installed unique telephone and water systems in the days before electricity was available to them. World War II kept Colonel Storke away from Sebec for several years. When he and Mrs. Storke finally returned in 1950, they were welcomed home at a large party given at Packard's by friends from around the lake. (Carolyn Stecher.)

Tenting was very popular on Sebec Lake long before any camps were built. By engaging a guide, who provided all the necessary equipment, groups could spend a few days or weeks camping out at Tavern Spring, Greenwoods, or other choice locations along the shore. One of those who developed this type of business was Frank A. Jordan of Sebec, who used the large island in Buck's Cove (subsequently named for him) as a favorite spot to set up his tents. (Beth Cawley.)

Frank Jordan also owned a steamboat, the *Frolic*, which he used to transport his guests and equipment from Sebec Village to his tent sites. The *Frolic*, and later the *Fred and Eddie* (named for his sons), was available by the hour, day, or week for excursions and fishing parties. The following excerpt is from a letter Frank Jordan wrote in reply to Albion Dwight Gray, a client from the previous summer, who had inquired about hiring the captain for a large fishing party: ". . . I will work for you with my steamer for $5.00 per day—be subject to your orders from 7 am to 7 pm. If you want me to work over those hours I shall charge you 50¢ per hour for whatever time you keep me under steam. If you want my tents I will pitch them the same as last year and charge you 50¢ per day for the use of them, you to deliver them to me in as good condition as you receive them less the usual wear and tear. My canoe is sold so I cannot make terms on that . . ." Unique to Captain Jordan's campground on the island was a large revolving table, much like a Lazy Susan, which the guests turned to serve themselves. When Jordan moved his business to Great Pond in the Belgrades, he continued to use the revolving table, which was set up under a permanent gazebo on Oak Island. (Dick Jordan.)

In 1890 Willis E. Parsons, a Foxcroft attorney, bought a lot at the lake and began construction of a cottage which would become a local landmark. Parsons, impressed with the castles he had seen during a trip to Europe in the 1880s, decided to build one for his new wife, the former Miss Agnes Gilman. A large flat boulder 50 feet wide and 15 feet high served as a foundation, and Granite Mountain, which loomed behind the site, formed an appropriate backdrop. The tower with its observation platform 60 feet above the water could be reached by climbing a ladder from the third floor. The building's exterior was sheathed with tongue-and-groove wood siding scored vertically to simulate stone, and the dimensions of the battlements over the kitchen area were made smaller than those on the front to make the castle appear larger from a distance. He named his summer house "Norwood" (for North Woods), but because of its unusual design, it became known simply as the Castle. A shield above the entrance bears the "Norwood" name, as well as Agnes Parsons' initials. The stone battlements along the shore were made from 2-by-2-by-4-foot granite blocks, and were probably quarried locally. The wall itself was destroyed by ice during the winter of 1912–13 and was not rebuilt; the stones remain scattered along the shore. It is said that Willis Parsons built the Castle for $1,200, using French Canadian laborers. (John Parsons.)

The steamer *Marion* docked at the Castle, c. 1903. Built in 1887 for Marion Atkins and David Greeley, this boat operated longer than any other steamboat on the lake. During her forty-five-year career the *Marion* was controlled by three different owners; she survived a fire and was rebuilt; and when she became unsafe, her last owner, Harry Coy, sent her to the bottom of Buck's Cove, where she lies today. Sitting on the dock are Agnes and Willis E. Parsons (holding his son, Willis Gilman) and an unidentified guest. (John Parsons.)

In this photograph, taken on Katahdin's summit c. 1929, Willis E. Parsons (top) stands with a group of hikers including his son, Willis G. (in front with binoculars). The elder Mr. Parsons was Maine's first Commissioner of Inland Fisheries and Game, serving from 1918 to 1929. During his tenure he helped to establish several conservation measures designed to protect Maine's fish, game, and natural resources, including the single-deer-limit law, state fishing licenses, and the 90,000-acre Katahdin Game Sanctuary. (John Parsons.)

The view from Granite Mountain was spectacular and well worth the climb from Packard's, as this young lady with the binoculars suggests. At the turn of the century the mountain had far fewer trees than it does today, and was covered with blueberries. Steamboat captains advertised excursions specifically for those wanting to pick berries and picnic at one of Sebec Lake's most popular spots. (Biri Fay.)

A hike to the Ice Caves, a jumble of boulders between Granite and Ragged Mountains, produces a cool reward for very little effort. Numerous people have enjoyed climbing under and over the rocks where ice a foot thick can often be seen in July. The cool air coming from deep in the crevices is a welcome relief after a hike up the trail. Perley Arnold, Walter Arnold's brother, is seen emerging from a cleft in the rocks, c. 1910. (Beth Cawley.)

Edward J. Mayo, business manager of his family's large woolen mill in Foxcroft, was among the prosperous business and professional men who built cottages on the lake in the 1890s. Inland Maine, in keeping with a national trend, was experiencing a return-to-nature movement at this time, and many people were constructing their own private retreats on the state's freshwater lakes. Many of the camps built during this period are still held by the original families. (Stuart Hayes.)

Theodore Wyman's speedy *Anamosa* is dwarfed by Edward Mayo's *Waban* at the Mayo dock in the Greenwoods section of the Big Lake. The *Waban* was christened *Ivy F* when it was built by Marion Atkins and David Greeley, but the steamer was renamed by Colonel Mayo when he purchased it in 1901. A few years later, George Thompson put the *Waban* back into public service, running excursions from Greeley's Landing to the head of the lake. (Dave Raymond.)

In 1922 the Mayo camp was sold to Harriett M. Balcom, a nurse, and Ethel L. Sargent, a teacher, who turned the property into a girls' camp. Wichitee, Camp of the Warblers, sought to give its clientele an outdoor experience with emphasis on physical activities such as swimming and canoeing so that the girls might "be prepared to meet more successfully the restrictions of ten months in the less natural life of our schools." The campers slept either in bungalows, open and screened on three sides, or in tents with raised platforms. Wichitee's campers spent much of their time exploring the area around Sebec Lake, taking hikes to nearby mountains, canoe trips and picnics to South Cove and Jordan Island, and steamboat excursions from the head of the lake to Sebec Village. Camp brochures assured parents that their girls would be met at North Station in Boston for the train ride to Dover, and that their baggage would be conveyed safely up the lake by Harry Coy. Parents wishing to visit the camp were urged to stay at Packard's. Although Wichitee was well-run as a happy and healthy experience for the campers, as a business it failed, closing after six years. The photograph above shows the property as it looked in 1925, with the main camp surrounded by various outbuildings which have since disappeared. The boathouse at the left was later moved to another camp Colonel Mayo owned below the Narrows. (Stuart Hayes.)

This delightful couple enjoying a game of cards is Hanna (Lane) Gray and her husband, Albion Dwight Gray. The couple lived in Philadelphia, but spent summers in Maine at their home in East Sangerville. Dwight Gray especially enjoyed Sebec Lake, and for a few years in the 1880s he joined the fishing trips run by Captain Frank Jordan. Mr. Gray signed up his friends from Philadelphia, who wanted to camp on the lake for several weeks, while Captain Jordan provided the tents, boats, and gear. (Biri Fay.)

In 1890 Dwight Gray bought Deer Point from the Adams brothers, and soon after, he and his wife's family, the Lanes, built two camps on the North Shore. The one on the left burned shortly after it was built and was not replaced. The one on the right (now Fay) was used by the Grays to entertain family and friends, many from the Philadelphia school where Mr. Gray taught. (Biri Fay.)

Dwight Gray died suddenly in 1896, but his wife continued to come to Sebec Lake, converting the camp with its additional cabins into Camp Schönwasser, a summer retreat for the girls at the school where she worked. Each year she returned to her East Sangerville home in the spring to prepare for reopening the camp, but according to this postcard, written April 10, 1907, she found everything "under the largest drifts of the winter . . . I left the city of brotherly love a little too soon." (Biri Fay.)

Ellen Hooker shows off a nice catch of fish at the Gray camp in 1910. She and her sister Alice were old family friends of Hanna Gray's, and the girls often spent time at Sebec Lake. When she died in 1929, Hanna left the camp and the farm to Alice and her husband, Sidney Davidson. The camp was called Graylane by the new owners. (Biri Fay.)

Alice and Sidney Davidson (standing) and a group of family, friends, and assorted pets have their picture taken on the porch at Graylane Camp, c. 1940. Among those assembled are the Davidson's daughters: Louise (left), Alice (center, holding kittens), and Jean (far right). Additional sleeping quarters, guest camps, and various outbuildings had been added by the Davidsons over the years to accommodate their large family and the constant flow of summer guests. (Biri Fay.)

Sidney Davidson Jr. behind his father's ChrisCraft, c. 1940. Water skis were not used on Sebec Lake until the following year, when Sir Harry Oakes brought a pair with him from his home in the Bahamas. The wealthy Sir Harry hired Francis Smith and Earl Crossman to take him around the lake behind Frank Smith's ChrisCraft. In addition to paying the boys the princely sum of $10 per hour, Sir Harry also gave them the skis. (Biri Fay.)

These women from South Shore are enjoying a visit to Gibraltar, c. 1933. From left to right are Bertha (Crankshaw) Redman, Annie Peaks Kenney, Elizabeth "Bill" Brown, and Emma Crankshaw. Gibraltar has always been a popular destination for Sebec Lake boaters. Privately owned for a number of years by the Davidsons, Gibraltar and 14 acres surrounding it were given by the family to the town of Willimantic in 1972 for use as a public park. (Gini Redman.)

Judging from the smiles, the girls from Camp Wichitee are having a good time at their cookout in South Cove. The white sand beach was always a favorite picnic spot. Francis Peaks, who owned most of the land around South Cove, gave 800 acres, including the beach, to the state of Maine for a park. It was dedicated in 1964 in memory of his parents and his sister, Annie Peaks Kenny, who, he said, "loved the lake like no other place." (Stuart Hayes.)

Stephen Orman Brown assumed ownership of his father's woolen mill when he was just twenty-six, and successfully operated the business for thirty-two years. S.O.B., as he was affectionately called, bought half of what is now known as Brown's Island in 1889, and started his camp soon after; he acquired the other half three years later. The Brown camp has had several outbuildings and tent platforms added over the years to accommodate S.O.B.'s descendants, who still enjoy summers at Sebec Lake. (Madelyn Betts.)

These young ladies from Dover pose for the camera at the Brown camp. Members of a literary group called the Book Club, the girls were having an outing at the lake when S.O.B. snapped this photograph of his daughter Celissa (second row, third from left) and her friends at the big rock in front of the camp. The only other person identified is Annie Peaks (second row, second from left). (Elizabeth Brown.)

64

Theodore H. Wyman of Sebec built this camp soon after he purchased his beach lot in April 1889. Named Birch Lodge, it was the first camp constructed on the South Shore above the Narrows. In the 1890s the original camp (above) was turned so that the gable ends faced east and west. A large porch was added to the front of the rearranged camp, resulting in its present look. (Dr. Edwin Wyman Jr.)

Theodore Wyman's fascination with steamboats led him to experiment with engines and boilers, and to come up with several small steamers for his private use. Two of his earlier models, shown at the Wyman camp before the turn of the century, are the *Trout Fly II* (center) and the *Restless*. Working with steam boilers had its drawbacks, however, and Mr. Wyman's efforts were not always successful. The original *Trout Fly* blew up! (Dr. Edwin Wyman Jr.)

Arthur and Jessie Howard and their children, Dorothy and George, weigh their chances of taking a canoe ride on a day when they have to hang onto their hats. In the days before outboard motors, northwest winds made travel in small boats difficult along the South Shore. The Howard camp was built in 1900 and was the last of the original twelve camps built in this section of the Big Lake. (Georganne Dow.)

The girls in Dot Warren's Tri-Hi-Y group spend a weekend camping out at Howard's, c. 1955. No power lines travel up the South Shore, and the camps are only accessible by boat. The Howard camp, like several others nearby, has a main building surrounded by a cook house and sleeping cabins. These girls, who have set up camp on the living room floor, are: (clockwise from the top) Sylvia Richards, Alice Bickmore, Dot Warren, and Georganne Howard. (Author's collection.)

A sense of community has developed among the families with camps on the South Shore, above the Narrows. The twelve original buildings were built between 1889 and 1900, and many are still retained by the initial families. Generations of children have grown up fishing, swimming, playing cards, and running the path that connects the camps, while adults have enjoyed the annual Shore Picnic and swapping stories on the wide open porches characteristic of these old-fashioned camps. No road access and no electricity keep many things the same as they were one hundred years ago, with careful consideration given to each modern "improvement." These South Shore residents gathered on the beach between the Howard and Wyman camps, c. 1935. From left to right are as follows: (front row) Orman Brown, "Bill" Brown, George Howard, and George Doore; (second row) "Eli" Schoen, Arnold Norcross, Cellissa Norcross, Annie Peaks Kenney, and Rachel Barry; (third row) Eddie Howard, Millie Whitacre, unidentified, Bertha Redman, Jessie Howard, Dot Howard, Ned Schoen, and Arthur Howard; (back row) Alec Barry, unidentified, Jane Barry, Lucy Barry, John Redman, and Francis Peaks. (John Redman.)

In this 1928 photograph, Edwin P. Sampson prepares to take a spin in the *Florence*, the gasoline-powered boat named for his wife. The Sampson camp was built c. 1893, when Mr. Sampson was principal of Foxcroft Academy. He and his wife left the area a few years later, but returned in 1920 to retire. When the couple died, the property was left to Mrs. Sampson's sister, Bertha Crankshaw Redman, whose family still spends summers at the lake. (Gini Redman.)

This is one way to take a shower at Sebec Lake. Virginia (Redman) Shepherd pours water over Sam Jr., in spite of her son's loud protests. Generations of the Redman and Shepherd families have come to the lake, and Sam Shepherd Jr. and Elizabeth (Redman) Brown have compiled a genealogy of South Shore families, a result of all the conversations "on the porches, in the cookhouses and around the fireplaces [about] who was related to whom and when certain branches of the family were active at camp." (Gini Redman.)

As a young man, Eugene Barry came to the Lake House in Willimantic to hunt and fish. While attending a dance at the spool mill hall, he met Lucy Wyman (sister of Theodore Wyman), who had come up the lake with other young people from Sebec. Their marriage brought them to the Wyman camp on the South Shore, and led to their ultimate purchase of the nearby Kittredge camp for their own use. This is a fifth generation camp. (Elaine Balsley.)

Francis Peaks is shown here aboard his sleek naphtha launch, the *Sis*, c. 1910. Named for his sister, Annie Peaks Kenny, the *Sis* was used as a pleasure boat, and was often seen traveling between Greeley's Landing and the Peaks camp, built in 1897 on the South Shore. Around the turn of the century the highly flammable naphtha was used as a fuel in small boats of this type, but because of its high volatility, use was limited, and only a few boats on Sebec Lake were ever powered by it. (Dave Raymond.)

John G. Mayo, prominent Foxcroft businessman, had just built this fine cottage on the South Shore when this c. 1890 photograph was taken. Mr. Mayo also constructed a granite pier in front of his camp to accommodate his 30-foot naphtha launch. Before 1900, several piers of this type were built from stone cut close to the lake, perhaps at the Merrill quarry on Davis Mountain or at sites such as the one near the Hugh Barry camp in Tim's Cove. (Peg Padgett.)

Harry and Maude (Mayo) Bentz came to Sebec Lake every summer from their home in New Jersey. Mrs. Bentz was a daughter of John G. Mayo, and had enjoyed summers at her parents' camp since she was a young woman. Descendants of the Bentz and Mayo families still spend summers on the South Shore. (Sam Lamb Jr., John Lamb.)

This group of South Shore youth dressed as pirates may have participated in a boat parade held during the Regatta at Greeley's Landing during the 1930s. From left to right are Betty Buck, Jane Hall, Dot Voorhis, Pat Hall, Betty Herley, Dot Kibbe, Bob Leavitt, Florence Redman, Lucy Barry, Ted Barry, and Betty Hall. Dr. C.C. Hall's boat, the *Wawa*, is not to be confused with another boat by the same name, owned by Dr. Hall's son, "Buzz." The second *Wawa* was a lifeboat from a U.S. Navy destroyer. (Gini Redman.)

"Buzz" Hall and a friend put the finishing touches on the *Buzzzz*, a homemade wooden boat the young man built c. 1930. It was powered by a Mercury outboard motor, which sent the lightweight craft skimming along the water at speeds which thrilled the teenagers and provided them with entertainment for most of the summer. (Clair Hall.)

Wainwright Cushing, who started his career as a dyer in the woolen mills in Sebec and Dover, began to develop his own non-fading dyes after the Civil War. They were so successful he started his own company, and over the years Cushing Perfection Dyes became known all over the world. One of Foxcroft's most successful businessmen, Mr. Cushing was also one of the most generous, sharing his success and wealth with his community and its institutions. (Madelyn Betts.)

The Cushing cottage (now owned by the Jones family) was the site of many outings for veterans of the Civil War. Wainwright Cushing was proud to have served in that conflict, where he participated in several major battles and was wounded. An unselfish man, he was especially generous with his fellow veterans, often hiring a steamer such as the *Linwood* to carry G.A.R. members to his camp for daylong outings which included food, boat rides, and special programs. (Dave Raymond.)

In 1900 George W. Morgan and George P. Thompson built a three-story hotel on a point of land just above the Narrows. The hotel was not accessible by road, so guests were transported from Greeley's Landing by the *Linwood*, a steamboat purchased by Mr. Thompson. Appropriately called the Grand View, the hotel was run for only a few years around the turn of the century. The small cottage to the right was later moved to the North Shore, where it sits today as the Murphy camp. (Beth Cawley.)

New Yorker Walter S. Crittenden purchased the Grand View Hotel from George Thompson c. 1911. The hotel was reduced to two stories and converted to a private cottage by the Crittendens. Friends from the head of the lake pose here on the lawn with the new owners. From left to right areas follows: (front row) unidentified and Walter Greene; (back row) Helen Williamson, George Williamson, Alice Williamson, Walter Crittenden, unidentified, Charlotte Crittenden, unidentified, and Alice (Albro) Williamson. (Beth Cawley.)

A few camps on the South Shore at the Narrows were built around the turn of the century. Like the others in the Big Lake, they had no road access, and their owners had to row from Greeley's Landing, where their boathouses were located. They also rowed across the lake to a landing on the North Shore in order to buy butter, milk, and eggs at the Glover farm, or to attend functions at the Bowerbank Town Hall. (Steve Rainsford.)

Reverend Lyman R. Hartley relaxes at the Narrows in the 1920s. Though he was usually busy ministering to a large congregation at the Fort George Presbyterian Church in New York City, Reverend Hartley especially enjoyed visiting Sebec Lake in the summer. He was often called upon to lead religious services in Sebec Village and Bowerbank when he was at the lake, once delivering the re-dedication address to four hundred people attending the reopening of the Sebec Community Church in Sebec Village in 1927. (Steve Rainsford.)

"Dad" Warren came to Sebec Lake hoping to regain his health. He decided to live year-round at his camp at the Narrows, leading some to think he was a hermit. A thoughtful, quiet man, he occasionally guided for Packard's. He often had a social hour with the Rainsfords, frequently bringing Marion Rainsford a bouquet of wildflowers or some other little nature gift. Apparently Sebec Lake agreed with him, for his health did improve and "Dad" Warren lived an additional twenty years. He died in 1937. (Steve Rainsford.)

75

Baby Bill Rainsford, held by his mother, Marion, gets his first boat ride in the summer of 1910. The Taylor/Rainsford camp was built in 1899, and was bought a few years later by Joe Taylor, the popular local band leader. Marion, the only daughter of Joe Taylor, inherited the camp, and with her husband, Guy Rainsford, brought the family every summer to the Narrows. (Steve Rainsford.)

Guy Rainsford Jr. ("Nip," on the left) and his brother Bill help "Dad" Warren cut ice at the Narrows in the 1930s. No large-scale commercial ice harvesting was done on the lake, but the sporting camps and several individuals cut small amounts for their own use. The Rainsford brothers harvested the ice using hand tools, and transported it on sleds to an area behind the camps, where it was stored in sawdust. (Steve Rainsford.)

Four
Greeley's Landing

In 1858 Andrew Blethen plunged into the wilderness north of Foxcroft to clear land for a farm and a water-powered sawmill. Blethen's Mills, at the outlet of Bog Brook on Sebec Lake, was marginally connected to civilization by a hand-hewn road which originally came through Foxcroft Center. As steamboating on the lake became more popular, people began traveling this road to meet the boats, which stopped at Mr. Blethen's wharf. By 1879 a livery stable was added near the wharf, for the convenience of those enjoying a day on the lake, and when David Greeley came to the area a few years later, his various businesses created so much activity that the place gradually became known as Greeley's Landing. Sawmills, a boarding house, and even a school (the white building, center) made Greeley's Landing a busy neighborhood before 1900, when this photograph was taken. Note that the road had remained little more than a wagon track, however. Francis Peaks later moved the schoolhouse to the shore near the steamboat landing, where it functioned as his boathouse for several years. (Tim Merrill.)

In 1885 David Greeley put up a large steam-powered sawmill at Blethen's Landing. He had contracted with Lucius Dwelley to provide the spool mill in Foxcroft with white birch, an enterprise that required mill and woods crews as well as several teams of horses. Just four years later, they were hauling 35 cords a day from the lake to the mill. Greeley and his partner, Marion Atkins, also had two steamboats built, the *Marion* and the *Ivy F,* which increased passenger service on the lake and activity on the shore at Greeley's Landing. (Tim Merrill.)

The Blethen farm (now the Log Lodge) has seen major renovations over the years, and today hardly resembles the prosperous farm it was over one hundred years ago. The twenty-room house, with its stable, large barn, and numerous outbuildings, has been owned by several people, including Marion Atkins, the woman who figured so prominently in the activities around Greeley's Landing at the turn of the century. Sawmill crews and woodsmen stayed at feisty Mrs. Atkins boarding house-and reportedly kept one eye on her parrot, which had the run of the place! (Francis Smith.)

Gorham Brawn bought the property in 1920, and spent the next several years farming, selling milk, and working with his horses at Greeley's Landing. The neighborhood school across the road had closed by this time, so the Brawn children had to travel 4 miles by horse and wagon to Foxcroft Center for their education. This picture of Gorham Brawn and his children was taken c. 1922 at their farm. From left to right are Eva, Edna, Gladys, Earl, Mr. Brawn, Alice, and Bertha. (Eva Mountain.)

In 1898 the shore near the steamboat landing was lined with boathouses belonging to families with cottages in the Big Lake and the Narrows. The storage buildings housed every type of watercraft, from steam yachts and naphtha launches to seaworthy rowboats and canvas canoes. Nearly all the boathouses are gone today. (Tim Merrill.)

Most of the surviving images of Sebec Lake steamers and their passengers are posed photographs, but this one, although old and faded, is alive with the activity surrounding a departure. One can almost hear the whistle blow as the passengers with their picnic baskets and extra coats climb aboard the *Morning Glory*. Whether testing the water, searching for just the right seat, or straddling the deck rail, these busy travelers provided plenty of action for this perceptive photographer. (Dave Raymond.)

Taking a cruise meant relaxing, enjoying the scenery, or getting caught up on correspondence, as Rachel Barry seems to be doing. Most of the steamboats would stop at private docks if prior arrangements had been made, and many camp owners and their guests preferred to travel this way. Certainly women dressed in turn-of-the-century fashions must have been more at ease riding in the relative comfort of a steamer than sitting in the family rowboat. (Elaine Balsley.)

America's love affair with the automobile was just beginning when this photograph was taken, and with easier access to the lake and more people staying at their camps, Greeley's Landing was becoming quite popular. Encouraged by all the activity, Harry Coy built this pavilion in 1922. Originally used as a dance hall, the building had a fine hardwood floor, a large porch overlooking the lake, and electric lights furnished by a Delco system. (Priscilla White.)

The steamboat pier in the 1920s had a portion of its deck covered for passengers' comfort. It was also a place to store the dry wood needed to fire the boilers on the boats. The *Marion* lies at the end of the dock while Jean Mason (Hilmar,) the little girl in front, waits with friends from New York for a ride to the family camp at the Narrows. (Steve Rainsford.)

81

From the early 1900s through the 1940s, Harry Coy was a familiar figure to camp owners and tourists alike, as he shuttled people and goods around the lake in the days before telephones, good roads, and reliable outboard motors. He carried lumber to build camps, mail, food, supplies, and maintained passenger service to the hotels and sporting camps. A captain of both steam and gasoline-powered boats, Harry Coy had a career on the lake that lasted more than thirty years. In this photograph he stops at Graylane camp to pick up Treat Davidson. (Biri Fay.)

Utilizing an early model pick-up truck, Harry Coy transported all sorts of goods and equipment from Dover-Foxcroft to the lake. In later years his trademark beach wagon performed the same tasks. Carroll Tyler, who sometimes worked on the boats with the captain, talks things over with Harry's son Des, c. 1934. (Eva Mountain.)

The *Marion* had the longest career of any steamboat on the lake—nearly half a century. This boat survived a fire in 1901, was rebuilt (with 10 feet added to her length amidships), had three different owners, and ended her career in dramatic fashion by going to the bottom of Buck's Cove "with full steam up." The original 35-foot *Marion* was named for Marion Atkins, who occupied the farm at the Landing. The *Marion* was faster than Ansel Crockett's second *Rippling Wave*, and the two boats competed keenly for business in the 1890s. When Harry Coy bought the *Marion* some years later, the steamboat rivalry continued with the Crocketts' successor, Willie Clarke. In addition to carrying mail, passengers, and freight, most of the lake steamers began the season in the spring by bringing down the booms of logs from the Big Lake. The boats were usually busy from ice-out until early fall, and many of them worked on the lake for many years. By the early 1930s, the *Marion* began to show her age; her boiler was old and her decks were rotting. After careful consideration, Harry Coy called his friend, Bill Rainsford, and the two took the steamer to a secluded area in Buck's Cove, bored holes in the hull and sent her to the bottom. After a recent article about the *Marion* appeared in the *Piscataquis Observer*, Pauline (Davee) Hitchings wrote, "I well remember the night Harry Coy took the *Marion* up the lake with lights all ablaze. We sat on the porch and wondered where he was going . . ." That night signaled the end of an era: the days of steamboating on Sebec Lake were over. (Des Coy.)

After scuttling the *Marion*, Harry Coy went down to the coast to look for a new boat. He brought back this fishing vessel and removed its marine engine, which did not suit him. Bill Levensalor, who owned a garage in Dover-Foxcroft, had salvaged an 8-cylinder Buick engine from a wreck. He quickly installed it in the new boat, and Harry was back in business. The mail, freight, and passengers continued to be carried on Sebec Lake until the mid-1940s, when Harry Coy retired. (Dave Raymond.)

In the late 1930s, Thompson Guernsey purchased the Brawn property, replaced its exterior with log siding, and transformed the old farm into a rustic retreat for New York businessmen. Originally called the Sebec Lodge and Aircamp, over the years the recreational facility became known simply as the Log Lodge. It was open year-round, and offered its guests a variety of outdoor activities, including horseback riding and swimming in the summer, and ice skating during the winter. (Bob and Ruth Weatherbee.)

The outdoor skating rink was surrounded by an ice wall. The blocks of ice were cut by hand in the cove and stacked several rows high to offer skaters protection from the wind coming off the lake. Inside, the lodge was equipped with furniture taken from the Mount Kineo House, which was being torn down at the time. (Bob and Ruth Weatherbee.)

In addition to renovating the farm, the company also built a bridge over Bog Brook and made several other purchases at Greeley's Landing, including the pavilion and the white sand beach (now the public beach). The entrance to the Beach Club advertised beach chairs and tables, diving float, tennis courts, bath houses, and protected parking. The beach even boasted electric lights, which ran off a battery-operated system at the lodge and pavilion, but the wire was strung such a distance the bulbs "barely glowed," according to those who remember the facility. (Madelyn Betts.)

85

The Lodge operated a flying service to shuttle guests from New York and Boston directly to Sebec Lake. One of the largest aircraft used was this seven-passenger, twin-engine, amphibious Douglas Dolphin, which generally attracted a group of delighted onlookers when it landed or took off. Sometimes the guests were flown to remote fishing sites in smaller float planes or to Greenwood Pond, where they then made the trip overland to the lodge on Borestone Mountain, which Thompson Guernsey also managed. (Francis and Marion Smith.)

The resort attracted the attention of several corporate executives, and some well-known celebrities, including Eddie Anderson, better known as "Rochester" on the Jack Benny Radio Program. When celebrities arrived, it was usually a much publicized event, and photographers lost few opportunities to snap pictures. "Rochester" was photographed ice skating (he had never worn a pair of skates before), sipping a cold drink sitting in a beach chair on the ice, and "calling Mr. Benny" on the lodge telephone. (Ellen Keenan.)

Sebec Lake

New York to Vacationland in 3 hours

Sebec Lake - Beach Club

... SEBEC LAKE ...
Summer and Winter Resort Camps
Seaplane Base *in the*
Maine Woods and Lakes Region

Trap Shooting at Sebec Lake | Ice Racing and Hockey in Piscataquis

For Reservations ... Write or Phone

RECREATION INC.   **MAINE AIRWAYS CORP.**

Advertisements in New York newspapers and other periodicals with large circulations were designed to draw guests to the Sebec Lake retreat. The B. & A. Railroad's annual publication displayed this full-page ad in its 1939 issue. The company soon ran into financial problems, and the resort was forced to close its doors after operating only a few years. A change in ownership turned the various facilities at Greeley's Landing into new business ventures after World War II.

As it became more and more popular in the 1930s, Greeley's Landing was selected as the site of a three-day regatta sponsored by area businessmen. The event attracted large crowds to a boat parade, baseball game, refreshment booths, and fly-casting, canoe, and swimming events. Dot Dow (Warren) and two other young ladies from Brownville Junction and Milo pilot these watercraft to advertise mattresses for a furniture store. Equipped with 2.5-horsepower motors, these unusual "boats" were used mostly to shuttle young people from the beach to the "white boathouse." (Dot Warren.)

In the summer of 1940, "Bun" Palmer and her daughter Margaret ran a small restaurant (now the Bob Merrill camp) which specialized in seafood and steak. It was very popular, attracting cottage owners and people from surrounding towns, as well as two very special guests. But Sophie Tucker and Kate Smith ate their dinner, signed the guest book, and left before their young waitress realized who she had served. (Margaret Goulette.)

Another familiar face around the lake was that of Willie Clarke. He was captain of several steamboats, including the *Leola, Goldenrod, Edna,* and *Elsie,* and his last boat, the *Falcon.* A big man, talkative and enterprising, Willie Clarke had an ongoing rivalry with Harry Coy, as both men competed for business. Once, friends of Harry's arranged chairs, broomsticks, and raincoats on the deck of the *Marion* to make it look like a full load of passengers "just in case Willie had a spyglass trained on them." (John Redman.)

Willie Clarke rented a few camps at the Landing, and his wife, Avis, ran the Pleasant View Tea Room, which served dinners. There was also a small store in the front of the building which catered to the needs of campers. Several local girls spent a summer or two working for Mrs. Clarke as waitresses, storekeepers, or berry pickers. Avis Clarke (center) poses with two guests, Mr. and Mrs. Leroy VanCleef, in 1941. (Francis and Marion Smith.)

Bob Weatherbee holds up a couple of salmon he caught through the ice in front of Dick Libby's camp in 1944. In the days before snowmobiles, power augers, and down parkas, ice fishermen were a hardy lot. Putting on snowshoes and hauling gear on a toboggan to the middle of a windswept lake for a day of fishing tested the resolve of many a Maine angler, especially after he cut several holes in 20 inches of ice with a weighted ice chisel. (Bob and Ruth Weatherbee.)

Bob Washburn helps dig out the car he and his friends buried in drifts on the lake, c. 1940. It used to be a favorite pastime among young men in the area to see how far they could travel on the snow-covered lake without getting stuck. Winter roads flagged with branches often crossed from Greeley's Landing to the Bowerbank shore, and travelers had to be constantly aware of ice conditions. Thin ice was responsible for several accidents on the lake. (Francis Smith.)

Sebec Lake Ice-Out

1879-M8	1899-M4	1919-A24	1939-M11	1959-A28	1979-A28	
1880-M6	1900-M 1	1920-M8	1940-M10	1960-M2	1980-A23	
1881-A28	1901-A22	1921-A17	1941-A22	1961-M3	1981-A14	
1882-M8	1902-A1	1922-A21	1942-A29	1962-M4	1982-M6	
1883-M4	1903-A17	1923-M6	1943-M8	1963-A28	1983-A20	
1884-A28	1904-A4	1924-A29	1944-M5	1964-M1	1984-A28	
1885-M11	1905-A29	1925-A23	1945-A10	1965-M1	1985-A27	
1886-M2	1906-M8	1926-M10	1946-A27	1966-A26	1986-A24	
1887-A28	1907-M5	1927-A21	1947-M6	1967-M4	1987-A13	
1888-M12	1908-M5	1928-M8	1948-A30	1968-A28	1988-A24	
1889-A24	1909-M9	1929-M3	1949-A15	1969-M5	1989-M2	
1890-???	1910-A20	1930-M1	1950-M2	1970-M7	1990-M1	
1891-A26	1911-M6	1931-A14	1951-A21	1971-M7	1991-A30	
1892-A30	1912-M 4	1932-A27	1952-A24	1972-M14	1992-M7	
1893-M12	1913-A27	1933-M1	1953-A17	1973-A27	1993-M2	
1894-A28	1914-M9	1934-A26	1954-A30	1974-M15	1994-M2	
1895-A29	1915-A25	1935-A28	1955-M1	1975-M5	1995-A24	
1896-M4	1916-A25	1936-A28	1956-M6	1976-A28	1996-M 2	
1897-M4	1917-M7	1937-M5	1957-A27	1977-A28		
1898-A28	1918-A26	1938-A27	1958-A24	1978-M8		

(A-April)   (M-May)

Ice-out is a hot topic of conversation in the spring. In recent years it has been the subject of a contest in which the winner receives a cash prize for correctly guessing the date and time the lake becomes navigable from Packard's to Sebec Village. Ice-out was more critical one hundred years ago, when loggers and steamboat captains eagerly waited for open water, so they could begin towing winter stockpiles of logs down the lake. (Bob and Ruth Weatherbee.)

"First in" is the rallying cry of those young and brave enough to jump into Sebec Lake in the early spring. There is no doubt about Earl Annis' claim to the honor in 1944—it was only February and the ice was still in the lake! The first swim was often taken at the "white (or tin) boathouse," the former Mayo boathouse at Greeley's Landing. (Bob and Ruth Weatherbee.)

Earl and Ethel Cole lived year-round at the Landing. This was on the west side of Bog Brook, where the public boat launch is today. Earl ran the marina, and Ethel had a lunchroom in one room of their home. Gruff, independent, and prone to speaking his mind, Earl Cole became an institution at the lake in the 1950s; and for those who remember him with a chuckle, echoes of his booming voice and colorful language still linger around the docks at Greeley's Landing. (Georganne Dow.)

When Thompson Guernsey's resort failed in the 1940s, the various segments of the business were divided up among several owners. Frank Smith retained the Log Lodge, the Town of Dover-Foxcroft took over the beach, and Frank and Virgie Allen bought the pavilion. In 1949, the Allens installed a new rock maple floor, and then opened the doors for roller skating. Rollerland attracted large crowds at its special skate nights, including the annual Miss Rollerland Contest. The Allens often sent hand-colored, mimeographed postcards such as this to their regular patrons. (Frank and Virgie Allen.)

SEBEC LAKE
ROLLERLAND
GRAND
OPENING BALL
FRIDAY
June 1st.
Skating 8-11
Adm. 60¢

Novelties–Favors
Door Prize!

Improved Floor..
Improved Skates..
Best of Music..

SKATING SESSIONS
Every
FRI. & SUN. 8-11
And
SUN. MAT. 2-4 PM
(Sessions will be altered
AFTER GRADUATION.)

Closing Ball at SKATELAND
in Hartland..Memorial Eve.

Starting in the 1930s, swimming lessons were given at the Greeley's Landing beach (now the Dover-Foxcroft public beach) and have been sponsored by various civic groups over the years. Andy McSorley, Clara Swan, and Lee McKusick were a few of the early directors of these programs, which not only taught children to swim, but provided summer jobs for young people around the lake who were hired as instructors. These beginning swimmers take advantage of the Red Cross swim program in 1945. From left to right are unidentified, Georganne Howard, Mary Bearce, Ethel Fairbrother, Maxine Lougee, unidentified, and Mary Gellerson. (Dot Warren.)

In 1917 W.F. Runnals (left) and his son Clair paddled their canoe all around the lake looking for just the right spot for a camp. They chose land near the mouth of Cotton Brook which Lyman K. Lee had offered for sale. There was no road to that area of the lake at the time, but the lot had a rocky beach and a good view of the farms and cleared fields on the Bowerbank shore. The first camp built on the property was struck by lightning in 1921, but it was rebuilt the following year. Today it is known as the Danforth camp. (Priscilla White.)

Will Runnals was an able mechanic who ran a machine shop in Dover. He was eager to find a lot on the lake because he needed anchorage for the *Ida Jane*, a boat he built himself and named for his wife. Clair Runnals built a camp on the point lot east of his father's in 1936, and the two families were often seen cruising the lake in the *Ida Jane*. From left to right, Charlotte Runnals, Sylvia Burgess (her sister-in-law), and Mrs. Runnals daughter Doris prepare to cast off at the dock in front of the camp. (Priscilla White.)

Five
Bowerbank and the Lower Lake

The town of Bowerbank was originally T7 R8, and like Willimantic, it was bought and sold in large parcels before settlement began. Early pioneers, crossing the lower lake from Sebec in the 1820s, cut back the forest to establish their farms. They set up a sawmill and gristmill on Mill Brook, and started a school and church in a small settlement away from the lake. When the inhabitants attempted to vote in Sebec and were denied—because they refused to pay a poll tax—they formed their own town. Granted a charter in 1839, the settlers named their town after Thomas Bowerbank, an Englishman who was one of the early proprietors. But the municipal burdens soon became too heavy, and in 1869 a petition for the repeal of the charter was granted by Governor Joshua Chamberlain. Bowerbank became a plantation in 1888 and was reincorporated as a town in 1907. Around the turn of the century, a few camps appeared on the Bowerbank shore between Seymour Cove and the beach (Levensalor's). Tavern Spring, near the beach, had been a popular tenting place for years, and steamboats often stopped there. It is said that Ella Perham, who lived near the end of the main road, walked down through her pasture in the evening to hang a lantern in the wooden structure to the right in this photograph, as an aid to navigation. (Biri Fay.)

During the years Bowerbank remained a plantation, residents paid their property taxes to the state. Mr. Charles Hesketh's 1889 tax bill of $3.50 for 367 acres of land seems like a bargain today. A story is told about a determined Bowerbank tax collector who once rowed up the lake to the South Shore in order to collect an unpaid tax of 50¢. (Rodney Preble.)

In the 1920s, Bowerbank Town Hall was the scene of some lively town meetings. Hot topics and hot tempers were so common that people from neighboring towns flocked to the town hall to watch the proceedings, and on several occasions sheriff's deputies were dispatched from Dover-Foxcroft to keep matters from getting out of hand. In sharp contrast to the stormy town meetings were the fairs, suppers, and sings, as well as the religious services conducted in the building by Miss Helen Corbett and the family square dances initiated by Dr. Edwin Wyman. (Madeline Acker.)

The Charles Clarke farm on the main road was one of a few large farms in Bowerbank with acreage bordering Sebec Lake. As the lake developed, Charles Clarke, along with George and Mattie Glover (who moved in later to care for him), sold parcels of land along the shore which had suddenly become more desirable for camp lots. The farmhouse, now owned by Rodney and Eunice Preble, still stands, although the large barns and outbuildings are gone. (Rodney Preble.)

George Glover loved horses and spent most of his life working with them. In a work diary kept in the early 1920s Mr. Glover recorded the various jobs he did each day in Bowerbank. He yarded logs, built bridges, graded the state road, plowed gardens, cut hay, hauled rocks, gravel, wood, grain, and lumber—all with horses. His journeys took him chiefly to Dover and Sebec, always by team. In the winter he crossed the lake to Greeley's Landing on a road over the ice. (Madeline Acker.)

On top of the hill beyond the Charles Clarke/George Glover farm stood the well-known William Glover place. Two of Mr. Glover's daughters, Adele and Mary, maintained the farm, selling milk, eggs, and churned butter to residents and cottage owners alike. No trip to camp was complete without a stop to chat with the women at the Glover farm. (Frances Tucker.)

Just beyond the farm. on a road to the shore, stood the small frame building Adele and Mary Glover ran as a tea room in the 1940s. They walked up the road from the farm with freshly baked goods every day. After the war, Bill and Frances Tucker operated the tea room, expanding the services to include home-delivered baked goods and ice for camp owners. This group of family and friends at the tea room are, from left to right: (front row) Daniel Johnson, Mattie Glover, Mary Glover, Genieve (Glover) Johnson, Florence Dobson, and Benjamin Dobson; (back row) unidentified, Adele Glover, George Glover, Arthur Lyford, Charles Clarke, and unidentified. (Madeline Acker.)

This small building close to the Glover farm functioned as the post office and store for many years, and although still standing today, it is almost entirely hidden by trees. Mary Glover served as postmaster from 1921 to 1963. A dedicated member of her community, Miss Glover also volunteered her time to the village school and other civic organizations. She once told a newspaper reporter, "Bowerbank, to me, is the finest, dearest spot on earth." (Madeline Acker.)

The Dow farm was located a few miles north of the settlement, at the end of a gravel road. This rambling set of buildings was surrounded by two large barns, sheds, and several acres of cleared fields. A.P. Dow managed the farm and brought up his family in Bowerbank around the turn of the century, but he was the last generation to do so. Roy Dow rented out the farm during the summer months in the 1930s, and later allowed hunters to use it as a hunting camp. The buildings finally deteriorated and the forest reclaimed the fields. Today, a few apple trees and cellar holes are the only remains of this back country farm. (Dot Warren.)

Souvenir

• Center School •

Bowerbank, Me.

Fall Term 1897.

PRESENTED BY

Louise M. Lanpher,
TEACHER

COMMITTEE
C. E. Glover   E. J. Donald
H. H. Clark   A. P. Dow

Pupils.

George Glover
Herbert Dow
Andy Moore
Johnnie Chase
Mary Clark
Lizzet Whittemore
Adele Glover
Elmer Glover
Elden Clark
Carlton Whittemore
Daniel Richards
Geneva Glover

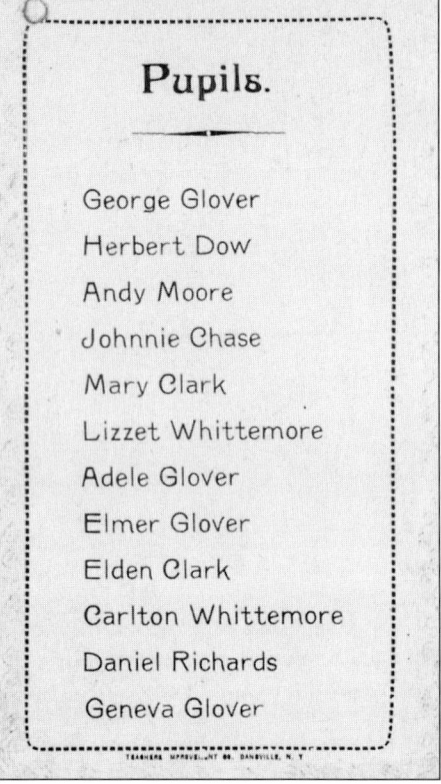

At one time there were three schoolhouses in Bowerbank, but eventually all were consolidated into the large Center School, located on the main road. There were usually from ten to fifteen students, taught by a teacher who boarded with local families. Bowerbank retained its own school until the 1920s. (Madeline Acker.)

Students at the Center School pose with their teacher, Mattie Glover, c. 1903. The only student positively identified is Adele Glover (the girl with the bow in her hair, back row). As it became increasingly difficult for the town to maintain its school, various members of the community participated as volunteers, even to the extent of bringing in a hot home-cooked meal for the students at noon. (Madeline Acker.)

Chris Preble, Bowerbank's well-known bear hunter, poses here with some trophies and the tools of his trade. Mr. Preble trapped bears weighing as much as 400 pounds, and was fond of telling stories of the hunt. He once caught a large bear in Lyford Swamp which had broken the chain and dragged the trap. Tracking the bear for three days to the Egery Quarry in Barnard, Mr. Preble finally found his trap—empty, at the top of a very tall tree. (Arlene Weymouth.)

Chris Preble's house sat on a hill overlooking the lake. Notice that when this picture was taken, it was possible to have an unobstructed view of Greeley's Landing across the open fields. There were many bear skins still hanging in the barn when Dr. Eugene Wyman purchased the property some years later, much to the delight of his niece and nephew, who came to spend summers with their parents, Dr. and Mrs. Edwin Wyman. (Heather Crozier.)

The uninhabited sections of Bowerbank have been heavily lumbered over the years. Logging camps and woods roads were scattered across the township and a Lombard log-hauler road once passed through it. Wildfires in the 1820s had destroyed thousands of acres of forest in central Maine, but sixty years later, the large stands of white birch which grew out of the devastation stood ready for harvest. Some of the most extensive timber harvesting in Bowerbank was done by the American Thread Company in Milo, which cut huge quantities of birch as far north as Buttermilk Pond. Men in large woods crews, working a specialty job such as swamper, chopper, sled-tender, or teamster, started early and stayed in the woods until 4:00 pm, when they returned to camp. Their noon meal was taken out to them by the "cookee," who might pull his sled a couple of miles to where the men were working. The meal usually consisted of baked beans, a biscuit (sometimes frozen), hot tea, and molasses cookies. The supper menu did not vary much from the noon meal, but the men got to eat it in the warmth of the bunkhouse. As one logger summed up his days in the woods: "You worked hard. Ate good. And was tired at the end of the day." The picture above was among several photographs given to the Sebec Historical Society by Mattie Glover, and was probably taken north of Sebec Lake. The young man to the right with the dog appears to be the cookee who carried dinner to this woods crew. The bearded man standing at center has been tentatively identified as a Mr. Levensalor, who lived in Bowerbank. (Sebec Historical Society.)

Around 1900, a few camps began to appear along the North Shore below the Narrows. In 1906 Oliver Kemp, a New Jersey artist and illustrator, bought a small camp near Seymour Cove. Using fishing and hunting themes inspired by the local area, Mr. Kemp provided illustrations for the covers of *Harper's*, *Scribner's*, *The Saturday Evening Post*, and other magazines with a national circulation. His cover for the 1914 Bangor and Aroostook Railroad's annual publication is typical of his well-known illustrations. (Beth Cawley.)

In June, 1943, a workboat caught fire below the Narrows as it was towing a large boom of logs. Camp owners on the Bowerbank shore offered to help put out the fire with buckets of sand from Levensalor's beach, but the men decided to cut the boom free and sink the boat before it could drift ashore and cause damage. (Neil Soule.)

Around the turn of the century the McKenney family, who lived in the Boston area, began to spend summers tenting at Mrs. McKenney's parents' farm in Charleston. The young family enjoyed this activity, especially when a permanent wooden building was added as a cook house. But in 1903 they decided to try tenting on Sebec Lake. They packed their belongings in a wagon and drove to Sebec Village, where they boarded a steamer which took them to a beach in the Greenwoods section of the Big Lake. It was such an enjoyable experience, the family returned year after year, sometimes tenting, and occasionally renting the Ham or Arnold cottage on Wilson Stream. By 1912 the McKenneys decided the Bowerbank shore was more appealing, and made plans to move their Charleston tent camp to a lot near Tavern Spring, which they rented for $10 per year. The family built a tent platform and an attached 14-by-16-foot cook house with a covered portico. This arrangement served them well for about ten years. The McKenneys later moved their tent camp a half-mile up the shore to the Crockett land, which they were able to buy. The floor and walls of the cook house were floated to the new site, the building enlarged, and a four-sided roof added. The result was the above structure, which was used by the family until 1950, when Clayton McKenney bought Piney Point (Timberoo) and sold the tent camp to Kenneth Campbell. The camp was one of the last examples of a sight that was once common on the shores of Sebec Lake. Mr. Campbell's nephew and wife, Dave and Diane Smith, are the current owners; they no longer use the tent, but have incorporated the original cook house into their present camp. (Dave Smith.)

Horace Morison's stern-wheeler cruises past Levensalor's beach in 1931. Mr. Morison was a lumberman who had used the steamer on Nicataous Lake to tow logs to his sawmill there. He moved the boat to Sebec one winter, a journey that took a week and tied up traffic from Sebec to northern Hancock County. As a young man, Roscoe Lamson fired the boiler on the steamboat, and was sometimes required to go ashore for more fuel so Mr. Morison could make it back to Sebec Village. The boat in the foreground is Bill and Ila Levensalor's *Pontiac*. (George Levensalor.)

In 1932 Walter Farmer decided to build a camp on the shore lot he had recently purchased from Charles Clarke. Trucking the lumber to Bowerbank and down the only existing road to the shore (through Ella Perham's pasture), he tied all the materials together and placed a cookstove on top. Mr. Farmer was fond of telling his grandchildren how he paddled his top-heavy raft down the shore to the campsite, always ending his story with "and I couldn't swim a stroke!" Walter Farmer's grandchildren, Jean (Rich), Phyllis (Foss), Neil, and Walter Soule sit in front of the camp that was named for them. (Neil Soule.)

105

Lord's Camps

Comfortable Cabins on the Bowerbank Shore of Sebec Lake

A brochure from Lord's Camps welcomes guests to the north shore of the lake, c. 1925. Jack and Ida Lord, who operated the main lodge and four smaller cabins during the 1920s and '30s, advertised good hunting and fishing, home-cooked meals, and relaxation at beautiful Sebec Lake. Open from June 15 to December 15, the camps were available by the day or week for sportsmen and families. After Mr. Lord died, Ida Lord continued to run the camps for a few years with her husband, Harold Kling, and her sister Maybelle. (Lois Reynolds.)

Sumner Ward bought three of the Lord camps in 1946, including the main building (above), which had served as the dining room. The camp survives today, with some additions and modifications, and is still owned by the Ward family. Dr. John Palen, who had been a guest at Lord's, also purchased one of the camps. (Lois Reynolds.)

In 1932 Dr. Harry Noonan, a Dover-Foxcroft dentist, bought a tiny island off the Bowerbank shore, opposite Parsons Landing. Using lumber sawed by Ira Doore and floated across the lake, Dr. Noonan built a camp perched high above the water. The camp's interior included a stone fireplace faced with rocks collected from the owner's geological jaunts. Note the bird's nest, fungus, and rose quartz on the mantel. Dr. Noonan was a sportsman, naturalist, and photographer, and his camp, like so many others around Sebec Lake, truly reflects the interests of its owner. (Marion Doore.)

On the opposite (south) shore, a short distance from the lake, stood the Parsons homestead with its large barn. As steamboating became popular, the Parsons family allowed people to stable their horses in the barn while their owners spent a day on the lake. (Susan Small.)

Around 1900, Anson and Annie Parsons began selling shore lots to a few local people, including Tom Sands and Wallace Dow, who eventually built camps. The Parsons then sold their farm and moved closer to the water where they lived in a small cabin at the top of a bluff. Part of this cabin is incorporated into the camp now owned by Nathan and Elaine Hall. With Mr. and Mrs. Parsons in this c. 1920 photograph is a neighbor child, Helen Preble, who spent much of her time with this kindly old couple. (Arlene Weymouth.)

This photograph of the camps at Parsons Landing was taken before 1920. The camp on the left was built by Tom Sands in 1913 (it is now owned by Bob and Arlene Weymouth). Steamboats stopped at the dock in the foreground to take on passengers, and because of shallow water, wagons filled with baggage and supplies often had to back into the lake to off-load their goods. (Arlene Weymouth.)

Standing on the steamboat dock, Ira Doore and his daughters Marion, Marjorie, and Verlie wait with friends for the boat to take them to their cottage. The trip by land from East Dover to Packard's began to be too tiresome (see p. 43), so the family traveled the 6 miles to Parsons Landing and rode the steamer instead. Eventually the Doores sold their Wilson Stream camp and bought land at Parsons Landing in 1921. The camp Ira Doore and his brother-in-law, Henry Towne, built on the site is still owned by Marion Doore. (Marion Doore.)

Swedish immigrants Oscar and Helga Peterson came to Bowerbank after World War II to start a sporting camp at the lower end of the lake. Operating from 1945 to 1963, with five cabins and a main lodge, the Petersons served some notable guests, attracted, no doubt, by the meals served by Helga and Marie Peterson. The dock area at Peterson's Lodge, which displayed both the American and Swedish flags, once appeared on the cover of *The Saturday Evening Post*, painted by guest artist Bill Schaeffer. (Madeline Acker.)

Fred Gates, Sebec's eccentric "hermit," lived near the lower end of the lake, where he farmed, raised a few animals, and managed very well with only an occasional trip to Sebec Village. He disliked "store boughten food," especially packaged bread, which he called "northwest wind," and warned, "Don't git into the habit of eating out of the store. T'will be the ruin of you." Fred often worked around the shore with his Holstein bulls and two-wheeled dump cart, moving the large rocks that mark Gates Landing today. He let his hair and beard grow long, went barefoot, and seldom wore a shirt in the summertime; his pants were held up with rope suspenders. But he was well read, had a wry sense of humor, and although he preferred his own company, he occasionally ventured over the hill to visit his neighbors, the Townes, at their farm (above). The late Pauline (Towne) Mallett, who grew up near Gates Landing, told wonderful stories about the hermit and his eccentricities: "Once a group of blueberry pickers, all women, wandered too far and were unknowingly trespassing on Gates' property. Suddenly they were terrified to see (in their own words) 'a wild man, half naked, running through the brush.' The neighborhood was roused, the area searched, but no culprit was found. When Fred heard the story, he only laughed. 'Like blueberries myself,' he remarked. 'Made a pie only yesterday.' " Another time "picnickers, who were frequent visitors to the beach in front of Fred's home, were invited up for a 'mighty fine stew.' When the meal was over, upon being congratulated on his culinary art and asked for his recipe, Fred led his guests out back where a cat skin was tacked to the wall. 'That's what's left of your dinner,' he said. Fred always chuckled at this point. 'Never did see them pests again,' he said, 'and it's a danged fool that don't know a rabbit stew when he eats it, just a danged fool.' "(Dave Mallett.)

Six
Sebec Village

During the first half of the nineteenth century Sebec Village bustled with activity. The 18-foot drop at the outlet of the lake allowed early settlers to harness water power for the first mills in the county. As the settlement grew, these mills became important to pioneers establishing homesteads in nearby Bowerbank and along the south shore of the lower lake. In 1812, Sebec became the first town in the county to be incorporated, and by 1820 it was the largest town, with 431 inhabitants. But by the end of the Civil War Sebec's fortunes began to change. Over one hundred men joined the Union forces in that conflict, and of those who survived, only a small percentage chose return to their home town. In addition to the loss of its young men, the village at the bridge was bypassed in 1869 by the Bangor & Piscataquis Railroad, which ran several miles away, along the southern boundary of the town. Declining population, changes in manufacturing and transportation, and increasing hardship on small family farms sent Sebec into an economic depression that lasted several years. But, like many other Maine towns faced with changes beyond their control, Sebec adapted as best it could. During the last half of the nineteenth century the lake became an important resource, as steamboating and tourism developed. Men like Ansel and Fred Crockett, Frank Jordan, and Ross Lamson kept alive the economic hopes of Sebec Village long after the industrial sector had disappeared. (John Parsons.)

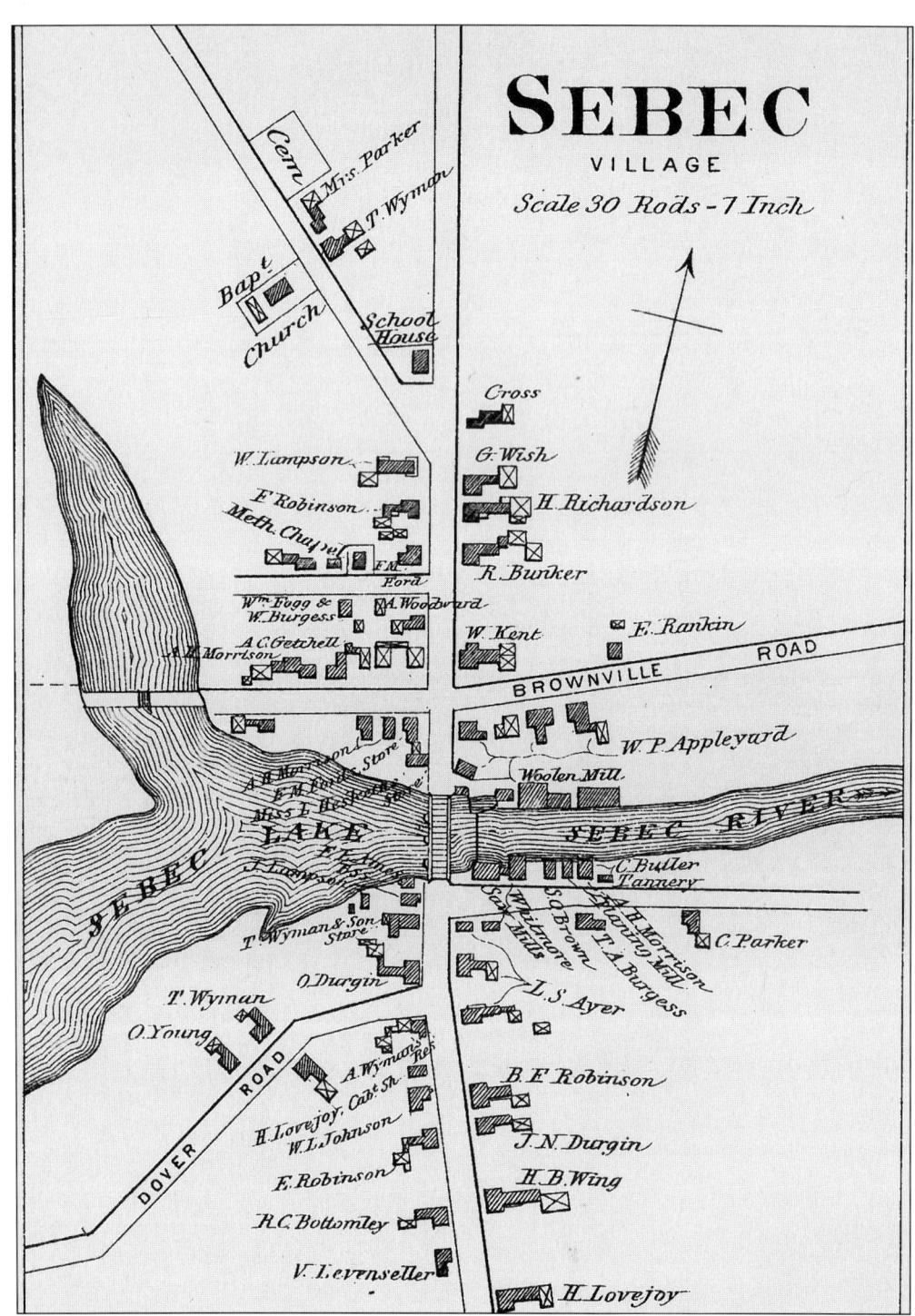

Although business and industry were already on the wane in Sebec when G.N. Colby's *Atlas of Piscataquis County* was published in 1882, there was still plenty of activity at the outlet of the lake. The Appleyard woolen mill was thriving, and sawmills, a planing mill, a tannery, and several stores and shops made this the town's center of population.

Mill owner William Appleyard, his wife, their son William (at left, being held), and daughter Iva (standing at left) pose for the photographer at their home in 1890. At the time, the mill was still profitable, but just a few years later the business failed, dealing Sebec another economic blow, and leaving citizens with bitter feelings toward the owners, who, they felt, had "let down" the community. (Sebec Historical Society.)

In this early-twentieth-century photograph, the mill buildings on both sides of the bridge have already begun to deteriorate. John Durgin's slab mill (left) and the Appleyard woolen mill were eventually torn down. The old wooden bridge was replaced by one of concrete in 1909. The small white building at the north end of the bridge was used at different times as an office for the mill and as a doctor's office. (Biri Fay.)

These young women, with their parasols and picnic hampers, are attending an informal gathering at one of the homes north of the bridge. Women at the turn of the century began to be increasingly involved with interests outside the home, and rural towns like Sebec saw them influencing and making contributions to the civic, cultural, and social activities of their communities. (Sebec Historical Society.)

The well-kept homes and businesses at the south end of the bridge made Sebec Village a picturesque spot around the turn of the century. John Durgin's sawmill is in the left foreground. Above it are, from left to right, the Wyman home, the hotel, the T. Wyman & Son store, the Joseph Lamson home—later known as the Ship House, a blacksmith shop, and at the far right, the Robert Wright home. (Biri Fay.)

A large crowd gathered at the church in Sebec Village on August 24, 1912, to participate in the town's centennial celebration. A program of music, reminiscences, and speeches by Stacy C. Lanpher, Charles W. Hayes, Major Wainwright Cushing, and other notables highlighted the festivities. Several historical artifacts were displayed in the school across the street, including a wedding coat and vest brought to town by Sebec's first settler, Ezekiel Chase. The church was originally Baptist, but later became a non-denominational community church. This building burned in 1953. (Elsie Watters.)

The largest school in the town of Sebec was this two-story building in the Village. It sat on the site of the present fire station, and served students in the area until the Harland A. Ladd School was built in 1952. After fire destroyed the Sebec Village Church, the school building was taken apart piece by piece, and the lumber used to build the present church. (Biri Fay.)

Although Sebec had clusters of population at the Village, the Corner, and the Station, the rest of the township gradually came to be settled by small farmers. Most people in Sebec in the late nineteenth century farmed to some extent, and a few owned large successful farms, such as this one on the Downs Road. William Downs purchased his land after returning from the California gold rush in 1852, and although the property did not quite reach the Sebec River, his 400 acres allowed him to have a diversified farm and to steadily improve the land. His success as a farmer led to his appointment as a manager of the Experimental Station at the Agricultural College in Orono, and his home was the site of the first Grange meeting in Piscataquis County. The farm, with its adjoining barns and sheds, is a classic example of the connected farm buildings that were unique to northern New England. Behind the main house were a summer kitchen, a buttery, a cold cellar, a harness shop, a tool shed, storage areas for hay and grain, and separate barns for dairy cows, horses, and sheep. Only the house remains today. Like many nineteenth-century back country farms, the barns and sheds have tumbled down, and most of the fields have grown up to woods. (Mac Blanchard.)

People in rural communities have always relied on each other. It was common around 1900 for farmers to have husking bees, barn raisings, and to help each other cut hay and gather crops. Even in the 1940s men worked alongside their neighbors to cut up the winter's wood. Roscoe Lamson (second from right) is using his portable saw on the Cove Road with help from Guy Stone, Clyde Nason, Gordon Stone, and Kenneth Lancaster. (Elsie Watters.)

In the same spirit of cooperation, these men dig out the Mead-Morrison snowplow, which had become buried in drifts on the North Road, c. 1944. The drifts on the road were so deep and hard packed even the old plow with lags on the rear could not get through. From left to right are Quinn Livermore, Bert Huff, George Green, Jim Nelson, Charlie Green, Ray Davis (rear), Will Towne, and Aubrey Mallett Jr. (Mac Blanchard.)

Music was an important part of community life around the turn of the century. Nearly every town had a band that gave public concerts and played at special events. Band concerts and steamboat excursions became very popular at the lake in the 1890s. In this combination the steamer *Favorite* teams up with Damon's Fife and Drum Corps from Barnard. (Madeline Acker.)

This photograph of Taylor's Band was taken in Sebec Village c. 1868. One of the most popular musical groups in Piscataquis County, the band was started by Hinchliffe Taylor (third from left) and also included his talented son Joe, who was about ten years old at this time. When Joe Taylor moved to Dover as a young man, he became active in the musical affairs of the community, playing, conducting, composing, and teaching music until his death in 1927. (Steve Rainsford.)

After Ansel Crockett sold the Lake House to B.M. Packard in 1894, he moved to Sebec Village and continued to run the *Rippling Wave II*. The rivalry persisted with the owners of the *Marion*, and, in fact, increased with the launching of a new Crockett boat, the *Goldenrod*, in 1899. Sixty feet long and powered by a 25-horsepower engine, the *Goldenrod* cruised along at 8 miles an hour with Ansel's son Fred at the helm. Graceful and distinctive with her yellow cabin, she was a handsome addition to the Sebec Lake fleet. *Goldenrod*, like most of the other lake steamers, was used as a workboat in the spring. Lumbermen usually made towing arrangements with the boat captains prior to the log drive, and as the following letter suggests, some of these men had developed a comfortable working relationship over the years:

Orono, Maine. Apr. 2, 1904
Mr. Fred A. Crockett
Sebec, Maine

Dear Sir:
Just through an old habit and for the sake of something to worry about, we are going to drive some logs across Sebec Lake. Although I have not said anything to you as yet, I would like you to be on hand with your Tow Boats as soon as we reach the Lake and help us in every way you can to get across. As we have a short Drive into Onawa Lake, we expect to get into Sebec Lake much earlier than last year. Awaiting a favorable reply. I remain Yours truly,

[Signed] Thomas Gilbert
(Sebec Historical Society.)

A lone river driver picks his way across a jumble of logs above the dam in Sebec Village. This was a common sight around the turn of the century after steamboats brought down the booms from the Big Lake. From here the timber was sent down the Sebec River to the Piscataquis and on to the mills along the Penobscot. Many of the logs went to Howland, and in later years most of the pulp went to the St. Regis mill in Bucksport. (Dr. Edwin Wyman Jr.)

A narrow opening in the boom let the logs into a channel, where men guided them to the sluiceway. Temporary wooden walkways built behind the dam made the work easier, but these sure-footed individuals were just as competent on a rolling log. The white building is the powerhouse, which was destroyed by fire in 1946 and was not rebuilt. The present hydroelectric facility did not become functional until 1984. (Roscoe Lamson.)

After the American Thread Company moved from Willimantic, it used a Lombard log hauler to transport white birch to its new mill in Milo. Powered by steam and steered by a man who sat out in front of the engine, the log hauler towed six sleds, each loaded with 6 cords of birch, for a total of 36 cords per trip. Once in awhile, one of the daring young woodsmen would stand on the runners of the last sled for a particularly hair-raising ride to town. (Madeline Acker.)

The log hauler road, as well as some of the woods roads, were iced to make the heavy loads easier to transport. A sprinkler was fashioned from a wooden box mounted on sleds and pulled by a team of horses. Roads remained usable for several months when iced in this manner. In this 1918 photograph, men are using the horses to raise the water barrel in order to fill the sled. (Elsie Watters.)

The steam-powered log hauler snakes its way through Sebec Village, returning for another load of birch in Bowerbank. The log hauler road traveled up the south shore of the Sebec River and across the bridge in the Village. Turning left on what is now Cove Road, it proceeded along the north shore of the lake to the Buttermilk Pond area, 17 miles from Milo. Parts of this road have been incorporated into present-day camp roads. (Dave Raymond.)

Sebec Village residents experienced some anxious moments when the dam burst during the 1936 flood. Heavy rains in March sent torrents of water cascading from the lake into the river, and residents anxiously awaited the fate of the bridge as water poured around both ends of it. The biggest problem was the ice, as huge cakes came crashing into the bridge abutments. Men worked around the clock piling sandbags and diverting the ice, in some cases blowing up the largest pieces before they reached the bridge. Their efforts were rewarded; the bridge held, and was finally reopened after being closed to traffic for three days. (Elsie Watters.)

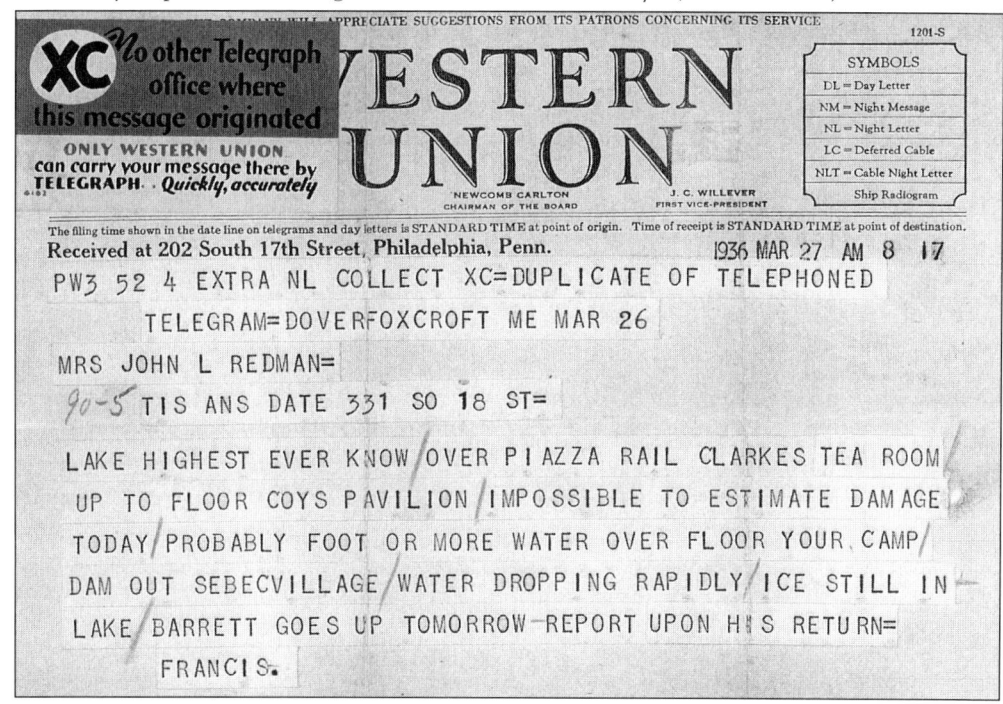

```
PW3 52 4 EXTRA NL COLLECT XC=DUPLICATE OF TELEPHONED
     TELEGRAM=DOVERFOXCROFT ME MAR 26
MRS JOHN L REDMAN=
90-5 TIS ANS DATE 331 SO 18 ST=
LAKE HIGHEST EVER KNOW OVER PIAZZA RAIL CLARKES TEA ROOM
UP TO FLOOR COYS PAVILION IMPOSSIBLE TO ESTIMATE DAMAGE
TODAY PROBABLY FOOT OR MORE WATER OVER FLOOR YOUR CAMP
DAM OUT SEBECVILLAGE WATER DROPPING RAPIDLY ICE STILL IN
LAKE BARRETT GOES UP TOMORROW REPORT UPON HIS RETURN=
     FRANCIS.
```

At the time of the flood Francis Peaks kept his South Shore neighbors, the Redmans, up-to-date on the effects of the high water. The flood caused widespread property damage around the lake in 1936. (Gini Redman.)

The popular Sebec House provided accommodations for many out-of-town people who came to the Village to spend a week or two in the summer. In addition to its twenty rooms, the hotel had a dance floor in the ell, and a large barn and livery stable in the rear. Ross Lamson, the proprietor, is the man in the wagon. The building was sold by Mr. Lamson in the 1920s, and was torn down. (Madeline Acker.)

These buildings between the hotel (extreme left) and the bridge are the T. Wyman & Son store, the Ship House, and the blacksmith shop. The Ship House was so named because of the extensive remodeling done on the first floor by Dr. Eugene Wyman to make it resemble a ship's cabin, complete with portholes, bunk beds, and the wheel from a ship. Dr. Wyman enjoyed letting his friends from the Boston area use the unique accommodations when they visited Sebec Village. (Elsie Watters.)

Theodore Wyman Jr. is shown in the Sebec Village store that he operated, first with his father, then as sole proprietor, beginning in 1880. T. Wyman and Son sold general merchandise from the building which still stands near the bridge. After Mr. Wyman died, the business continued to be run by his daughter Caroline until the late 1940s. (Dr. Edwin Wyman Jr.)

The Wyman children pose for the photographer c. 1893. Caroline spent all her life in Sebec Village; both Eugene (center) and Edwin later practiced medicine in Boston, but they always returned to Sebec in the summer and for holidays. A generous family, the Wymans gave much to their community. Eugene made a beach for Village children behind the Ship House, and funded Fourth of July celebrations, complete with watermelon and fireworks. The Reading Room and the Community Church benefited from the Wyman philanthropy, and many a Sebec child was treated free of charge by both doctors. (Dr. Edwin Wyman Jr.)

Theodore Wyman's experimentation with steam boilers resulted in a patent for his Wyman Safety Tube Boiler, which he used in building several steamboats for his private use. The *Restless* (above), as well as the *Anamosa* and the *Anamixis* (which were built for his sons), were all used by the Wyman family on the lake. The inventive storekeeper even fashioned a boat which used an automobile for power and steering, but this boat was not used in Maine. (Dr. Edwin Wyman Jr.)

Sometimes the *Restless* was hired for large group excursions, when one steamboat could not accommodate everyone. In 1899 the *Restless*, along with several other steamers, was employed when the American Woolen Company's Brown Mill provided a daylong excursion on the lake for its employees and their families. (Dr. Edwin Wyman Jr.)

Abner Morison's houseboat was a familiar sight on the lake, as its owner frequently motored to various sheltered coves to anchor for the night. Originally a steamboat, which was later converted to gasoline, the boat was a colorful sight with its potted plants hanging from the upper deck. Abner and Frank Morison were prominent Bangor and East Corinth businessmen who ran Morison Brothers, manufacturers and dealers in fertilizer and farm chemicals. Mr. Morison is shown entertaining guests aboard his comfortably furnished houseboat. (Madeline Acker.)

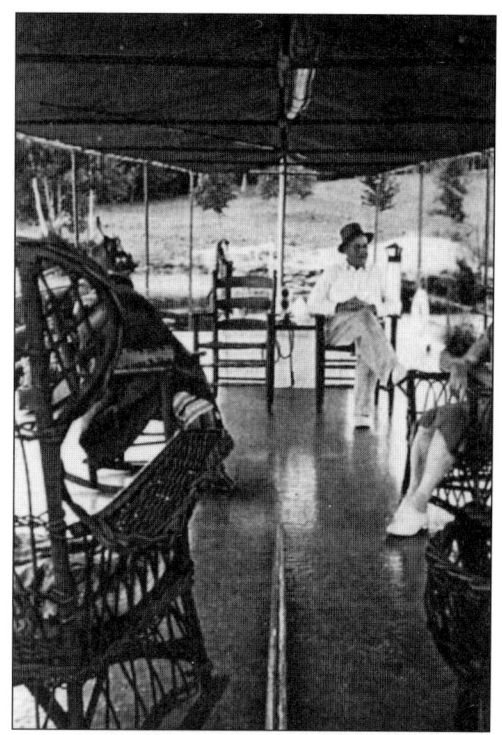

The Morison and Wyman families, who were distantly related, always spent the holidays in Sebec. In this 1940 photograph the two families share Thanksgiving dinner at the Wyman home. From left to right are Dr. Edwin Wyman, Edwin Wyman Jr., Lizzie ?, Blanche Morison, Abner Morison, Carrie Wyman, Alice Heather Wyman, and Katherine (MacKenzie) Wyman. (Heather Crozier.)

Few boats on Sebec Lake turn as many heads and draw as many favorable comments as the sleek, 36-foot *Anamosa*. Built by Theodore Wyman in 1900 for his son Eugene, the steamer claimed to be the fastest boat on the lake-and probably was, until she blew her boiler in 1916. She was then converted to gasoline and used by the Wyman family for several years, until the old boat was finally retired in the 1960s. Put to rest in a Bowerbank boathouse, the *Anamosa* remained there until high water floated her out into the lake in 1976, boathouse and all. Rescued from the flood and carefully restored by Dr. "Hap" Gerrish, the graceful old boat can still be seen cruising up the lake on a good day. As the *Anamosa* approaches her 100th birthday, she represents more than a modern maritime miracle. She is a comfortable link to the past, a reminder of the simplicity, the history, and the treasure that is old Sebec Lake. (Dave Raymond.)

Bibliography

Bicentennial, 1776 USA 1976. N.p.: Cosmopolitan Club of Dover-Foxcroft, ME, 1976.
Carey, Russell. *3,750,000,000 Perfect Wooden Spools*. Unpublished M.A. Thesis, University of Maine, 1994.
Haynes, George. *Souvenir of Dover and Foxcroft*. Dover, ME: Barrows, 1899.
Loring, Amasa. *History of Piscataquis County*. Portland, ME: Hoyt, Foss & Dunham, 1880.
Packard, Marlborough. *Packard's Camps, 1894–1916*. N.p.: 1974.
Roberts, Gwilym R. *Sebec, Maine Before, During, and After the Civil War*. N.p.: Maine Humanities Council, 1991.
Sawtell, William R. *Onawa Revisited*. Milo, ME: Paper Pusher, 1989.
Shepherd, Samuel G. Jr. and Elizabeth Redman Brown, eds. and comps. *A Genealogy of the Families Associated with the South Shore of Sebec Lake above the Narrows*. 2nd rev. N.p.: 1994.
Stevens, Louis E. *Dover-Foxcroft: A History*. Somersworth, NH: New Hampshire Printers, 1995.
VanHyning, Conrad. *Willimantic, Maine: Past and Present*. N.p.: 1976.
Wright, Shirley Nason. *The History of Sebec, Maine, 1812–1987*. Dover-Foxcroft, ME: The Piscataquis Observer, 1987.